Tunes of Time...
Incessant You

Vishal Sarkar

BLUEROSE PUBLISHERS
India | U.K.

Copyright © Vishal Sarkar 2025

All rights reserved by author. No part of this publication may be reproduced, stored in a retrieval system or transmitted in any form or by any means, electronic, mechanical, photocopying, recording or otherwise, without the prior permission of the author. Although every precaution has been taken to verify the accuracy of the information contained herein, the publisher assumes no responsibility for any errors or omissions. No liability is assumed for damages that may result from the use of information contained within.

BlueRose Publishers takes no responsibility for any damages, losses, or liabilities that may arise from the use or misuse of the information, products, or services provided in this publication.

For permissions requests or inquiries regarding this publication, please contact:

BLUEROSE PUBLISHERS
www.BlueRoseONE.com
info@bluerosepublishers.com
+91 8882 898 898
+4407342408967

ISBN: 978-93-6452-008-9

Cover design: Yash Singhal
Typesetting: Namrata Saini

First Edition: March 2025

मैं अक्सर लिखता नहीं
(काव्य संग्रह)

*To,
Vishal,
Lots of Love & Happiness,*

विशाल सरकार

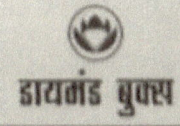

Shahrukh sir you wrote— "To, Vishal, lots of love and happiness."

Sir during the whole process you were engaged at least 7-9 seconds, and sir reason was me and my 1st book,

it was my great achievement sir.

Goosebumps on my achievement sir.

Love you too.

1 book is in Mannat,

another is in my hands autographed by you.

Sir I believe on my written words,

once written— "*Sabse bada shayar main hu,*

jise pata hai, ki tanhaiya'n kitni zaroori hoti hai...

isliye wo mashoor hona nhi chahta."

But from now my hustle is to be a name optimum to big enough, to write for you in films.

11 books I have already written... 51 stage performances,

2600 shers and just 2nd, Tunes of Time... Incessant You is coming, Genre - English.

It will be too signed by you sir... I believe for sure.

Will work brutally harder after this,

the date is marked... 11 February 2025 sir, my life changed sir.

Preface

This book is about every human emotion possible. Certainly, at this age, whatever I could cover,

I assure you I will not bore you; I will suffice to say, entertain, and emote you with my work and skills.

"Tunes of Times... Incessant You" is my second book, Genre – English,

after *"Main Aksar Likhta Nahi"* published in 2020, Genre – Hindi,

available on Amazon and Flipkart.

I will not, of course, do whatever I did with, *"Main Aksar Likhta Nahi."*

The problem with that was... due to some personal reason, I didn't promote my first book *"Main Aksar Likhta Nahi"* even to its lowest.

When it was launched on Amazon, Flipkart, on 20th, December 2020.

I was in bed on the 27th, 28th, 29th December, due to some inward sounds which amplified on to me,

or take it as normal as it could be,

but in those days, when being a published author (predominantly, it should be...

in fact, the elation, hangouts, and meetings), rather, when I went out,

I was the most awkward and pathetic person, I could be many, many times back.

A person whom even I would have scolded or thrashed, all internally and externally.

Because somewhere, whatever you write, it's not always your *kalpana*/imagination but actually the things which you are influenced by,

including the inclinations and effects too,

and somewhere, that was my personal diary which got published with my consent,

with my like all life's hue,

and literally then –

I didn't want to answer any questions like,

"*Meri cute cousin pr gya... meri respected XYZ, gym me aane wali har us khoobsurat devi pr, ya meri hone wali khushnaseeb wife pr.*"

So, I kept quiet.

Well... when you are a creative person, even being useless, every tiny bit or nuance of things should or does affect you,

and you should pursue the persistence,

just as you, not as you should be.

But as I had put great efforts into the craft for years and years,

in spite of being a master trainer in fitness sciences, I worked only for four hours and bore financial losses.

Now again, working is limited to evening for four hours, to write my second book, so it's a sheer waste of my efforts, my parents' hope, and of the publication who relied on me and the editorial team, only due to my personal useless concerns and reasons,

which are majorly hypothetical and imaginary meanwhile.

In fact, I was on Facebook then too, it was constant,

not a caprice, that for three-four months, after being a published author,

I used the "only me" option rather than friends/public for sharing my next creations.

Liking the popularity, in spite of that averse of popularity,

I was so scared of the response and attention,

the publication called my number,

they said, "Sir, for promotions, you should recite your book works on social media."

I said, "Sir, there are many calls and questions,

I can't bear these,

you do whatever from your side."

And the same people, known faces and personalities, whom I once feared, what they would think of my thoughts, with a person related or what questions might arise,

now ask the question "how many books were sold...??"

And this question became the game changer, I told myself – "Vishal, don't hinder...

with what you are personally."

So, after counselling from many beautiful people, and especially from my poetic idols,

I will be promoting my second book,

"Tunes of Times... Incessant You,"

to its fullest potential, whatever is possible.

And I promise, if I would not go mentally retarded,

due to overthinking, life would be easy and the form would be like the present,

then, for the upcoming 50 years of my life encompassing... 50 upcoming books,

intentionally intense, just casually,

and my skills developed throughout the process would be more enthralling... to you,

I assure you.

So, I am getting ready with my skill set already set, to hear from you...

"What a book... by Vishal Sarkar."

Thank you.

BUT WAIT WAIT...!!

IN THE WHOLE, THE MOST ABSURD WAS THE "CUTE+COUSIN"

IT MIGHT BE A TAINT ON AN AUTHOR'S BUILDING REPUTATION,

OOOH... WOW, WHAT A REASON I HAVE THEN!

I.e. AS THE CREATOR IS EQUAL TO EVERYONE...

SO, JUST BY TRYING TO SIT BESIDE HIS THINKING,

A CREATIVE PERSON SHOULD NOT BOTHER OR DISTINGUISH BETWEEN THE DIFFERENT SEEMING ANOMALIES... SO WHAT COUSINS,

THAT'S THE THING.

IF I WILL NOT OPT FOR WHATEVER BEST IS UPCOMING...

THAT'S CALLED HARM OR LOSS TO LITERATURE, NOW I AM BELIEVING...

BLAH... BLAH + BLAH... BUT I AM OK WITH IT.

BUT NO ONE HAS THE RIGHT TO ENGAGE ME OR TO CLAIM ABOUT THAT SINGLE GIRL EVEN WITHIN MARGINS...

WHOM I LOVED OR AM STILL LOVING...

I WANT TO GET RID OF THE SICK MENTALITY AND DELIVERANCE OF EACH OF HER BELONGINGS,
SHE WAS MY LOVE, IS MY LOVE... RATHER THAN THAT,

SHE IS A GIRL, SHOULD BE IN A SAFE ZONE, SAFE SIDE

TOO... NOT TO DEFAME HER,

AND LIKE THIS, FROM MY SIDE... THERE ARE MANY LIABILITIES,

THAT WAS THE REASON FOR ANXIETY.

WELL, WHATSOEVER, I AM A WRITER, I READ PEOPLE,

MY CONSENT OR NOT, NO ONE CAN DO THAT MUCH OF MY INTERNAL TESTINGS...

IF THAT'S SO...

THE EXCUSE IS THAT – I WAS IN A CHARACTER...

AND THUS,

I CAN CHANGE MY EMOTIONAL EMOTIONS LIKE AN ACTOR'S ACTING...

I hope so, that kind of adeptness is my emotional setting.

I hope you will enjoy reading it,

would go to the most appropriate page at the most appropriate time if one or two pages go averse to a belief,

just as I have written 2600+ works until now,

just if it went absurd and wrong, on one which you are reading,

it's like $1 \div 2600 \times 100 = 0.0384\ \%$ of mine,

i.e. not even making 1 percent of my thoughts, what I have entirely.

So, never mind.

And today I am at 2600+ poems, and I believe that, as has been seen,

the addiction to writing will continue until I die.

Definitely, with including my inclinations and developed mind, I am not boasting, but believe me, I am on this earth to write as a writer and poet, like not probably but,

I promise...

"AANKH K BADLE AANKH MANGOGE

TO EK ROZZ YE SARI DUNIYA ANDHI HO JAEGI"

.... By M.K. Gandhi

Like great lines 👍

Or even better than this, magically!
see the age difference!

Or even haven't used the superpower of alcohol or imbibed in even a drop,

like every time, one bottle down, the Great Ghalib.

So, sorry for the audacity or whatever with my efforts and tenacity,

thus, the developed mystics,

in the continuum, I am the greatest upcoming.
Then people will say, I am the resurrection of Rabindranath or Ghalib,

so, thus being at that state of mind,
I might claim,
whatever that is,
I am just from the field of literature,
again to serve the optimum, the maximum best,
the best harvest, and before that too the reaping.
Ok, ok... Hahaha...
take it as a joke, if it's hurting your sentiments,
you were like a slumber, sleeping,

I opened your eyes wide, with this audacity, and now mind-boggling,

I am just going averse of what,

I can be in serving the literature,
winning Nobel Prize or Booker Prize,
whatever to gauge the maximum parameters possible,
absolutely opposite to the feel of nothing.

Special Thanks

Special thanks only to the circumstances and situations.

Foreword

Nothing comes easy,
go do at least some crash course in English,
nothing you have to do,
just big-big dreams.
I will do this... I will be doing that,
you can't even talk properly.

Only the gist :),
of all in Bengali told by my great father,
Priya Brata Sarkar :).

Contents

To Modern Writers 1
Today Maybe I Am Nothing For Her, But One Day...
My Care Would Be Her Cure 2
An Ordinary Poem on Extraordinary Kaizzad Sir 5
Rest In Peace Kaizzad Sir 8
No Misogyny, But My Haughty Boss, Ma'am Chinmaya!! 10
My First Book Criticism Became The Genesis Of This Poetry 13
The Charisma Of Life 14
In Modern Times Alpha 15
Biographical Writing 17
Artist 20
I Adore And Revere You, With The Time In Charge
Nothing In Lieu Of You 21
Conclusion On The Way Coming 23
Think It 24
Women's Day Special 25
Omen 27
Pisa's Leaning Tower 28
Average To Near Mostly 30
What The Aspect Seems 32
When No Caffeine 34
1403 Kilometre Distance 36
I Being A Poet, You Helped Me, In Many Poems Of Mine 37
Hollywood 39
Every Bit Connotes Me To You 41

She Is An Addiction Undefined	45
A Nincompoop	47
Brahmos Missile	49
Conscious Efforts For You, Too Much Girl	51
Your Inclinations, Even Disturbs Me	53
Vishal Sarkar, The Best For You For Lifetime	55
She Gives Me Mental Stability	57
Tunes Of Time	59
If There Are No Add-Ons	61
I Am Gandhi	63
Grief's Optimum Auto-Correction	66
Bosses!! See Thus I Will Backfire	68
You Are A Goddess To Me, In The Religion Of Love	71
Why Not Only Me!!	73
With Everything, I Accept You	75
It's Sunday Morning Then Too	77
Percentage Of Receiving	79
Make A Proper Caret	81
Experiencing Hypoventilation	82
Verge Of Imminent End	84
I Am A Beautiful Person In All Syncs, Though Will Improve The Average	86
My Girl Is Going	88
Don't Bewitch Your Surroundings	91
It's Not People's Fault Actually	92
Feminism	93
Thank You2	94
It's A Human Psyche	95

I Am The Greatest	97
Anger! Many A Time Leads To Bravery And Many A Times It Drains Like The Internals	99
You Are An Active And Dormant Cutie	101
You Are Still Present Nearby With A Chance And Probablity In My Life	103
You Are A Catharsis	104
Rather	106
Global Patriot	107
I Am Running Better Than Your Brothers	109
You Are A Teacher	112
It Seems Like	114
Scent Of Sweat	117
I Will Presume Your Mental Health, Just Your Motor Units Misfired	119
Actually, Factually And Really	122
How Much???	124
It Is Happening	125
Strenuous Strides / Partial Killings	126
English Too Is A Superfine, Beautiful And Blissful Language	127
Penuiry Is Exactly Reverse To Divine	130
3 - 4 Hour Personal Time	132
No Rule Withstands	135
The Power Of This Piece	136
I Am Ready To Kill Or Die	137
English Shairy 102ish	139
Yes, I Am A Poet	140
Who Said Self-Doubt, Insecurities Are Not Good	142

I Am Tank Infront of Guns 146
Yes, You Are A Personality Development Course 149
No Feel Of Pro, Just Giving My Best, No Novice 151
Full Means Full, Complete Every Time, Even No Odd Or Ish ... 153
That's Why, I Am Showing 154
Dante Alighieri 155
Likewise 158
Include, Preclude, Conclude Or Exclude I Am Yours From
My Way Intrigued 159
Your Number Of Brothers Doesn't Matter To Me 162
Never Blame Yourself With A Lucky Tag 164
Thus, A Street Dog Seems Like An Injurious Lion Indeed
Without Doing Anything. 166
That's It Now, Abstract Things All Fallen In Pace 168
An Intresting New Year Journal Of 1-Jan-23 170
Nocturnal And Diurnal Both She Is And Will Be Contagious...
With All Days Not Even Excluding Me On Weekends
Or Sundays 171
The Slaughter House Becomes Gory 174
2 Years Old, Alan Kurdi Lying Dead On The Beach
(2nd - Sept - 15) Iraq And Syria War 181
It's Their Obvious View 183
Sometimes Actually The Response Is Not Bad 185
Vice Versa Conclusions 187
Life Is Not As Small As To Someone We Have To Write An
Impressive Letter 191
And There You Are At 3:30 Am 194
My Dream Olympics 195

The Nicest Thing About Gymming, Weight Training Or Weightlifting Is The Moment	198
It's His Problem	200
I Am Still Fiend Of You	203
Sorry, Don't Mind 😊	204
Sorry, I Was Inept To Find It	206
I Have Blinkers On My Eyes	208
With My Utmost Conscience, I Am In A Dim Sense Or An Innocent View	210
An Experience Which Usually Increases	213
Upto An Aeon You Will Always Be Precious To Me Just As Feeling For Life And Scars To Realize	215
Nevertheless	217
I Can Demean Me, In Myself	218
The Connection, The Vibes, The Anecdotes And My Internal State	220
When You Were Not A Mistress Of An Unfortunate Pea-Sized Brain	221
You Should Know Girl, From Then You Will Only Become An Evanescent Material In Me	223
You Cannot By Your Present Phase Overwrite Me	225
Maturity Is Not Suiting You	227
You Are My Olympic Medal For Lifetime Girl	229
Girl, You Were Impeccable, I Accept	231
18th Feb	233
It's Not Coincidently But Conditionally	235
I Am Anonymous For You It's The Accepted Truth To Me	236
But In The Religion Of Love I Actually And Absolutely Revered You	238

The Wetness In My Eyes Is The Witness That I'm Feeling You	240
I Am Knocking At The Door Delicately Of Your Heart So, That It Will Feel You But Won't Hurt You	242
Absurd Poetry But Not On Love	244
Because You Were Not A Short-Lived Desire Of Mine	246
See	247
5 Points Why Should I Select You	248
So Many Slogans On Aim	249
A Single Life	250
Failure	251
A Curved Path May Delay	252
Everyone Makes His Meal On Fire	253
I Was But Sorry	254
Hey Vishal!!	255
Like The Rain Drops Are Always Tangent To Their Sky	257
Thank You	259
The "Decibel" Of Sound	260
The Water Of Washed-Off Clothes	261
The Worst Story Told Of My Life	262
Every Sunset Has A Modest Feel For The Night	263
The In-Love Cuteness Of A Child	265
Revision Itself Is A New Course Of Persistence	267
We Don't Have To Narrate First, We Just Have To Make Our Stories	268
Better Are The Times I Show Not Even My Fangs And The Foe Persuades	270
So, Have Experience Of Humans, Yes Read Them	272
The Eureka Moment	274

When Meaningless Are The Altercations 275
Everything is Copied 276
Happy Mother's Day 277
You Are A Girl, Be In A Safe Zone, Safe Side 282
I Never Gloated You, Below Your Neckline 288
I Don't Write Generally *"Main Aksar Likhta Nahi"* In The Whole Lot, You Know A Jot Of Only This. 294
A Note From The Author 296

To Modern Writers

I cannot create anything,
in the name of creativity.

I have a standard in my lyrical meanings,
and what my words actually mean.

Otherwise, I too have the skills,
to describe even a cleavage in such,
a seductive form...
that...
it will seduce anyone than that of the actual representation of the boobs!!

But the belief on which I believe is,
that —
the touch and contact of pen with paper,
should create some feelings,
but not the lust.

Today Maybe I Am Nothing For Her, But One Day... My Care Would Be Her Cure

A girl different from the girly league,
applauded by me very much...
me being an ordinary boy,
maybe not taken seriously,
or felt the praises of a meek.
We are just friends...
she talks to me superfine,
but if a person is conscious,
he can even learn from a sparrow, or a squirrel too...
so, a student imbibed her bold behaviour,
being a girl, fearless, not a desk job holder,
but a bold dancer in public.
It's my New Year's resolution:
I will say, "Will you marry me?"
By consciousness, wealth, brawn instincts...
derived confidence one day, I guarantee.

As a spouse, I am imagining her and had done since long,
the remarks on her body parts,
her natural curves,
and still not being distracted,
and still proving...
is my motivation.
She has no fear in this manly world,
bravely increasing and inspiring,
the percentage of her minimal feminine others...
without knowing.

In a good way,
she showed me the way to be.
If I want her,
I should be an Alpha.
Otherwise, what's the point of even observing her or inculcating?
She showed me the way,
to dominate and intimidate my own boyish brethren and clans,
nothing but just if she is facing...
behind her back some abhorrent remarks,
as usual, rotten apples are increasing.
When my name will come with her,
she will be simply my girl.
No remarks no comments,
from now...
that's the work of my instincts.

Being a poet,
I am not so now, but earlier I was fearful on stage...
at the beginning.
(Credit from the beginning goes to her).
The day is imminent, soon I will be a famous name worldwide,
with all the influence and thoughts of her...
best part is,
while reading, she knows...
where my thoughts with the line are guiding.

One day I will be so omnipresent and big in her too...
that my care would be her cure.
For the world too... my genes would be certainly become sudden,
if given an egg fused with my sperm then nothing less than claimed...
best happening.

With Kaizzad sir
We will be proud always to use #builtbykaizzad as master trainers, love you sir

An Ordinary Poem on Extraordinary Kaizzad Sir

A Poem written on you, sir.
It's been two years, and I swear not a single day has passed that you didn't cross my mind :(
Date - 24-feb-2019
################

This poem I wrote for you, for my satiety, sir,
for you, sir.
Back then in class, a friend Shehrozz confided the confidential, you got to know,
I said I couldn't read my own words, I was shy,
and you read one-by-one, each word of mine, sir...
like this many words, phrases, sentences, and anecdotes are crossing my mind, sir,
you have given many students' lives a steady direction sir,
in those I am too one of the best sir...
that one year under you, 2019-2020, for becoming a master trainer,
was the best time for me sir.
Rest in peace.
Miss you sir.
####################

Weird face, with weird expression... because I didn't put on makeup,
I was not prepared for this, so that's why it seemed like an internal shake-up.
You seemed glad to have a click with me...
free in actions and smiling,
but on your one side, someone is heavenly happy within...

and is too nervous enough,
that, at the same time, suppressing an immature person who internally has brought up :).

But this photo, I swear, is the first I have with any celebrity, so proximal to myself,
that being a fan, I am not actually...
as I meet you often for studies as a student,
for being a future master trainer, sir,
and you are not someone who has come to the city for a short time or a day, and gone,
and die-hearted, I want a photo with you to click and hang it up.
But three days a week, 2019 – 2020, you will make the finest pottery from us, the clay.
I earned or by God's grace fallen into my part, or in an incompetent, you saw a competent fellow, whatever...
but as I don't know who said that - "*Guru ko bada uska shishya banata hai...*"
and as too I don't know for the same that how much I would be able to turn up,
every chance got, in the aura, ambience and presence of you...
because being a great opportunity, it comes with a big-big responsibility!

But sir, believe me, believe me, your respect in me,
It's like a 1 lakh rupees note autographed by you...
and I never use that even in my worst penury :).

Thanks for being my master...
and giving me an opportunity to relate myself to your prestigious institution called K11 Academy of Fitness Sciences...
and thus, giving me a hint that in this talented world, I am above mediocrity...

and with me and within me, sir, being you as an inspiration,
I can never falter,
even with my doomed, creviced, and folded destiny.

Rest In Peace Kaizzad Sir

My 1st book "*Main Aksar Likhta Nahi*,"
(Genre – Hindi)
IS SUCCESSFUL BY THIS ONLY :).
I wrote my book 📖 and didn't promote it due to some personal issues, as it happens,
with many authors.
I was uneasy about it to have any discussions,
like it's on Amazon and Flipkart, that's it...
it was my heart out and opened at many aspects personally...
but too on my master trainer friend and fellow's adamant request (Pawan Rahang), I was sending a copy to him, to the Pune K11 Branch and then thought if I'm sending it to him, then I will send it to Kaizzad Sir too... just like that... never expected anything...
and wrote a note including that "SIR, I KNOW THAT YOU WOULD NOT GET TIME TO GO THROUGH EVEN ONE OF ITS PAGES, BUT... IF POSSIBLE, JUST KEEP IT IN THE CORNER OF YOUR BOOKSHELF."
I knew you would pile it up with the invitation cards and other unnecessary accolades which you get hundreds each day, or your assistants will.
But today when you are no more, just yesterday... 13-October-21.
I went to Delhi K11 Branch for the prayer meet and after many talks, my fellow friend and master trainer Yogesh Sharma (now faculty) said:
"Do you know? Kaizzad Sir, read your poetry on *Maa* (which is on page 12), in the present ongoing master trainer batch."
I was shocked! I started to yell "*satch me... satch me...* " in breaks, 5+5 =10 times and in between Yogesh said "*haan bhai* " but like I didn't hear...
then again started "*satch bata rhe ho tum*" x times...

Yogesh got irritated and my second friend Himanshu Sharma confirmed "*haan bhai* ".

And said "*teri book sir ne table par rakkhi thi.*"

The book was released one year back sir, my words and that book would be here maybe after my life too, sir.

Never expected much from that book too, sir, but you recited my work in your voice three months back only, and I came to know today... is the greatest achievement of my book,

"*Main Aksar Likhta Nahi,*" sir.

I was unfortunately fortunate to know this, sir.

It brought tears to my eyes after coming home, enough big reasons and contentment included that I will continue to write till my end, sir.

I requested my fellow master trainer to have a click of that odd book wherever it is with your books and send it, I will frame it...

I know what it took from me to write that one "*Main Aksar Likhta Nahi,*" but never expected such a gracious enough behaviour from you, sir.

Proud that I was in the fifteen of the last master trainer batch of 2019-2020 which was trained by you, sir.

No Misogyny, But My Haughty Boss, Ma'am Chinmaya!!

I have been practicing and writing for approximately 12 years now.
May 2012 was when I commenced,
and made my first rhyme.

When I published my first book in Hindi,
"*Main Aksar Likhta Nahi,*"
I have changed many bosses...
one of my bosses said —
"By the money of "X-amount", and like bribe,
anyone can have it."
Then...
said to distribute it at an event...
(the event of her, where everyone was out of read or below mediocrity),
"It's trash."
She was ill behaved or ill; that's another matter, but...
but really!!
Proofreading, tallying, ink cost, paper cost, labour cost, mind cost,
editor charge, reader charge, ISBN,
Amazon, Flipkart handling, omnipresent Diamond publication
name... Its brand value,
the whole night of my jot, four hours of duty, half day for the library,
50% of earning already
forgotten for a mission for being entitled as an author,
being a master trainer, in spite of that, in too cheap shoes and cheap
outfits in front of junior personal trainers, she forgot it all!!
I was keeping quiet,
but I took it wholeheartedly, painfully,

because I respected her...
a bit more for being in this male dominated world with a genre of representing the women brethren and clans,
and engendering and supporting her female company...
(Including my bestie).
And yes, no job even in other gyms (1/2 for being an Author),
meant destitution.
That concept was too subtle,
but,
now when I changed my language to English,
and the work is in progress to publish my second literature, which is in English,
"Tunes of Time...... Incessant You,"
she the haughty must be opening a dictionary....
and tallying, being a high profile, top-notch, must be in conversation too...
then too... the English she never had.
She must not have learned so nicely till the 5th-6th class or maybe even later,
a word taken and when given by the teacher to use in a sentence,
her interest must be in another man.

And today, but today!
She must be astonished and flabbergasted...
that I take numerous times, like in a poem,
and use them all fabulously,
in a rhyme.
In this reminiscent mood, I can understand,
and after publishing the second, I will be much clearer...
that critic of mine,
was a lady who could not write her daily diary,
or even had the imagination being whatever read,
but...

to write more than, "My name is..."
It's hilarious.

And me with my own book in my hands,
what to summarize???
From me, whether seven years older, she apparently had also somehow enlarged brain.
What I have at present!
Her evaluation and revelation of truth by her,
Specifically, according to her,
why do I go into a zone???
Why was I surprised!
M.S. Dhoni went to make a six,
if I was there, I was making a four... (was not out),
being an averse example,
but a noob, librarian saying it, it's like.

But thanks to her, that it will fulfil,
my book with two pages and a guarantee...
I will forget her after this writing,
because on another topic I will spring,
but...
I will leave her dumbstruck again and again,
by my process and incessant future plans,
it's confidence-building,
without clearing clarified.

My First Book Criticism Became The Genesis Of This Poetry

A person who wrote a book of his own whole,
maximum time would be judged by those,
who don't carry the art or imagination of writing a single page.
A talent or hard work has much more criticism than the work of –
in nothing to engage.
Another thing is that you are not alike,
a cynosure is always a source of nit-picking,
like an endangered species, maximum times, it is never saved.
So, it's better to neglect,
and shine with the positivity and lustre of what you are made of and what you have got...
in your grabbed, thriving, and dominant phase.

Feeling weaker with the remarks of inferior...
who themselves never feel that "no one is lower or inferior to someone,"
should never be your case...

should never be your case.

The Charisma Of Life

The charisma of life to us is like suddenly
A barren land turned into a mesmerizing high tide.
The reference point (A) was set low...
very low! at zero like...
that's why we started with being strangers,
so, that we may feel the abundance,
like never before; nothing alike.
Girl, even after three decades on this earth,
thirty years!
Being strangers, anonymous was a tricky trick like,
otherwise!
The progress of indulgence in the graph,
with no way out,
under any circumstances, at all...
could be so exponential like 📈.

In Modern Times Alpha

Considering Google's definition –
"The dominant male/animal in a particular society."
But I would say just in any field or group of people with whom you sit,
you are culminating,
with reference points of the above,
in modern terms...
to be an achiever or Alpha,
an Alpha male or wannabe...
if thought properly,
the thought is already a fury.
In duration, in the making,
to tackle the storm is like it's already the dread and immense excruciating.
More equipped with weapons,
and detrimental are already there...
belligerent, with the arrogance of achieving,
plus, further, they are even more trying to benchmark devastation.
Any newcomer is a threat, in the incubation period and in the making.
To achieve something, it's already,
the suction of behaviour and mental sanity...
Alpha male... Alpha male,
the support system is there,
but most superiorly,
in the bad battle of life, it may be gory...
and it is a loss of total brotherhood and ingenuity up to infinity.
I too want to achieve the gory battle, what to do?
being first is not only about winning;
it is also about other Alphas' despondency.

From whatever the terms,
Sigma, Beta, Gamma, Delta are increment or uplifting or uprising only.
It's your negligence, but like closest to the nose of others, "Paraffin Wax," allergic stinking.
But whatever it's already going to be time's up,
in my father's aspect, I am a loser.
If someone says, "I will shoot you."
Said to Mom already, let it be...
it's the cost of dreams; of having.
I came to this new city not to continue the shortcomings,
I don't even want to be mediocre,
with fear and fear of pertaining,
eliminating all...
All fuel was, and still is, in to trespass the sophisticated, aligned boundaries...
I am a passenger rocket or missile, time imminent will tell,
what I am trespassing.
It's not mood-friendly,
but on trigger and dialect, purposeful declaring...
gory, abhorrent, bestial, or whatever friendly,
I am coming... coming... come what may!
Now winning is the only credibility of the spine containing.
Paramount enthusiasm is the new stability, in the process of my life good behaving.
In the continuum,
whatever the catastrophic seasoning,
but to myself and others,
hope so, at last:
Captivating, enthralling, and inspiring.

Biographical Writing

I am just a period apart...
I am fit for the fittest.
2400+ works, poems/dialogues, and still unable to crack Bollywood!
it must be no... not much quality, who said??
(Maximum who doesn't know how to write even a single page).
Yes, with minimal effort and some experience, many writers with 50-500 works, have cracked and done well.
But if a moron says, "concentrate on quality, not abundance or quantity, Vishal,"
I must say!
why are you then so mesmerized that, after 1000 efforts...
Thomas Elva Edison made the great bulb.
And the maximum effort after failure is still the great taste.
What were you saying??
If he did that after 20-23 experiments??
I am the grand greatest, I know...
better than great.
Properly ripen with no self-doubts,
envisaged.

When asked,
What will you do on 1st-January-23, New Year?
Someone said, "Party, we will celebrate with the best champagne,
or will you hang out with friends."
In my turn, I spoke:
"Today is my 1700th poem completing."
31st-December-22, I am on 1699 up to date.
Everybody said, "wow, whatever."

At 3:00 AM, 1st - January - 23, as said...
my 1700th came into my mind and then,
on paper by God's grace.
1900th... I completed it on 9th- June - 23.
So, as said,
1700th on January 1st is, by subtraction from 1900, is 200.
Thus, 200 works in 160 days is a quality slow pace.
One day, a miracle has to happen,
there is innumerable trace.
1900 in 11 years.
Each work takes five hours each,
1900×5 = 9500 hours.
I am not the biggest jibber-jabber,
my work is not a speck...
my work is my confirmed confidence.
'WRITER's BLOCK' definition and meaning -
"A non-medical condition,
primarily associated with writing,
in which an author is either unable to produce new work,
or experiences a creative shutdown with not many a time known case.
WRITER's BLOCK has various degrees of severity,
from difficulty in coming up with original ideas to being unable to produce,
work for years," damn whatever envisaged!
For me... what's that???
I have never experienced!!
1900 was just quantity, not quality...
what!!

I am always a run machine,
a never without form batsman...
it is the case with no breaks.
I am not demeaning or uplifting anyone,

everyone has their own aspects,
but you decide:
Sachin Tendulkar was great or Rahul Dravid was great.
When someone has made an agenda to demean or is in a condition of gaslighting others,
what is to be said???

Second book title "Tunes of Time,"
releasing in mid-2024, is baptized,
or was named in 2015.
Shows documented proof of a poem,
(to be published but never published),
indicates.
So, the dream following capacity of mine in a direction is over eight years...
four plus four, it is double engineering and above,
I am what I am, it all narrates.

Artist

So, the more he is bigger,
the more the community loses.
He never too wants the allegations of you,
"He is just a mediocre,"
and he wrote all those in a shallow dive.
It should be noted...
it should not be noticed,
for him, it's work time,
throughout the day.
Never mind!!
Artists never belong to attitude,
he lies down and surrenders, like...
whole totally to a zone and character,
don't complain of being neglected,
or that you are neglected.
You better be aware!!
don't intervene in the best coming...
poems, ideas, plays, phrases,
by changing him suddenly into a talkative mood or mindset...
the result would be,
with no probable probability even,
those lines will not interact with him ever like...
maybe never in his lifetime,
or hereafter will not even cross his mind...
due to inadvertently you!
it's a ruthless case, literature loses.

I Adore And Revere You, With The Time In Charge Nothing In Lieu Of You

I adore and revere you,
with every nuance and nicety,
added onto me with your experience.
Nothing like —
being special, then as every time available, so taken as granted and
simple are you!
Rather,
I am going to be better at loving you.
I experienced myself so far,
and observed in me inadvertently and advertently...
everything is practiced like to make an aura, atmosphere, ambiance,
and attachment best suited for you,
and around you,
and you are the solemn, formal, and dignified practice on my liking to
fathomless loving,
which all matters.
No distractions other than you,
nothing to entice or enthral,
like a person or an artist becomes a pro or proficient in some
performing arts by knowing the layers and nuances with practice,
I, with your proximity, coziness, and never-cloying attendance,
became what was to attain confident, classified class,
with your hand in my hand clasped,
to relish every nuance of you.
My love will never diminish,
as of now and so far,

if I break,
I will break into more and more satiety of being something known
exclusively to the art Girl,
more sparse,
with the time in charge...
with more ability to affect the surface area,
nothing in lieu of you,
hereafter rather than the,
repetition of you, no herald.

Conclusion On The Way Coming

To make me thankful by just suggesting the path,
like...
would be their successful taste.
With every enough and optimum cardamom, masala, veg, non-veg,
container, water, spatula, flame, etc., etc., all optimum,
I am already a celebrity in me and myself,
already I am a surefire method to succeed,
everyone would want to engage.
I am not seeking any verified profile, public figure, or celebrity,
some mental barriers are to be broken...
that, with so many coming acquaintances from them upcoming shouts,
praises to a cacophony,
how to manage?
And that's it,
you will see...
in the making,
who will be my godfather?
as their achievement first to attain,
at Bombay would be their race.
Conclusion on the way coming,
I would be the biggest name,
lower-class thoughts I do not belong,
I am a self-proved, self-made different case.
With brutality and calmness,
all in sync with optimum acceleration and power brakes.

Think It

Flawless is no one continuous ever, but...
Think about it, observe it, notice it, acknowledge it, and relish it!
More the major,
more this type of consequences.
Something is false in us,
from fathom to fathomless,
so that the correction,
or a sunshine's speck or a light at the end of the tunnel,
is to be shown or given, to thank someone!
and in gratitude then love being grateful...
even more that person more than normal.
It's a beautiful conspiracy.
Think about it!!
Otherwise, in a simple path in life...
that indulgence or that kind of indulgence was not possible.

Women's Day Special

A girl is weak and weaker than a man,
or me,
I was on a conclusion,
seeing you, observing you...
just as after hectic, strenuous work of days and days through...
limiting and omitting all,
most probably!!
I must have observed you when you necessarily needed to rest on weekends,
now it's the conclusion.
With less musculature and hormonal testosterone or T levels,
230 Kg deadlifts of mine versus yours 77.
Easy mobility of mine throughout 30 days in a month, and 365 days in a year...
versus you are restricted from prehistoric at every time by physiology to still every span,
you are like four days less like feeling your full potential,
then too you're 100 percent,
over yourself is your domination.
I envisaged what I was doing and claimed myself strongly, more specifically to other men...
you are out of competition.
Thanks, that way, that was my eureka moment!
for giving me a life lesson.
Thanks for showing...
by observing you,
got that very much you have to fight for day-to-day,
what you admire or you have ambitions,
because of us (males), everyone thinks of your security reasons.

Observing your hindrance and resilience,
I will be more as a man, stalwart and competent,
and the difference between the former me and the present me would be and will be,
at every glance, humongous huge,
with an uncomfortable, distinct distance forwarding me,
and others elimination.
Here is an example of you as a woman,
showing at least an equality equation,
that —
a spider web's string/thread...
is much more resilient and powerful in tensile strength,
in comparison to the same minuscule or girth of the same mass of stainless steel,
it's true, not for instance,
it is a scientific declaration.
Thanks for showing your eligibility neglected,
and the effect at every area of possible circumference,
and fighting against induced inhibitions,
with better emotions and intelligence.

Omen

Even up till when you are not ill,
or more specifically to the same ailment or disease,
you never know the same person's dilemma,
or even specifically how to care for or cure generally.
And thus, many a time,
illness and diseases averse to 'Holi' or other festivals,
wrapped in sympathy and empathy, makes a bond...
you never know!!
the beauty of being ill or someone's illness is just as good as the rest of life's togetherness,
with that recovered beautiful person,
plus, more when the erratic behavior and mood swings, on which or with which your calmness combined withstood,
drives and has a continuous sorry effect on them,
that magnifies the bond,
with the restored, revised and reformed relationship's different hue.
But don't be ill purposefully to see,
her withstanding nature or related grief and care for the same you.
I would say...
positively just love her,
no tit for tat to continue...
when a good and positive thing is with you,
negativity or related omen will not touch you.

True, it is too :).

Pisa's Leaning Tower

Whatever you are like...
thanks for the previous reference points in comparison to whatever you are with tunes of time,
abnormal things with their instincts,
many times, are much greater, soothing, pleasant to the eyes than the standard normal.
Like Pisa's leaning tower is inimitable, precious, greatest, and capable of enticing more as unique, being abnormal!! Being factual and real, whether or not...
every emotion related to you, even with mood swings and your devastating look and behaviour,
is unique as the noted and ongoing time.
Even so, like in humans rarely, you become unique out of mind, the cutest animal.
Thanks for taking out the monotony of the best subject
I want to study all...
every nook and free to move every corner,
being away from normal, delicious,
you are great then too great.

Same on main road views, not so...
from point A to point B, destinations,
daily the monotonous sweet-sticky daily journals!
But many times, the woods,
many times, mushy soils... unable to walk,
many a time what's wrong to muse on a decent park bench,
many a time contrast therapy of hot and cold with no interval,
many a times, intolerable tolerance,
everything you give with a destination.

Thanks for being with me still,
whatever the condition,
whatever the conclusion.

Average To Near Mostly

Life has ruined my other aspects,
but I still love you,
still crave you.
Without any recognition,
at the point dot,
like "He-Peacock" shows their unravelled, unfastened, untangled
feathers to "She- Peacock."
There at fields, all at once, without recognition or classmates!
She-Peacock chooses some with...
lavishing dance and mesmerizing, captivating overall.

I think if I was mere in honing myself in life, and...
what matters for your security most,
better I could have claimed you,
by default, I could have won you.
Intense love and care, whatever I had and I have still,
rather with just attraction and between a bit of love,
it might be a later part with you.
And nothing wrong!!
But,
with average to near mostly,
paralyzing all my actions,
like believing in and at only one doing,
since long been mesmerized by knowing you,
while standing stagnant and smiling in true love,
while slanting onto a wall,
or reclining on the sofa or bed,
I have just and just in true love...
cherished whatever got the memories,

and repeatedly... repeated you.
You were so mesmerizing, captivating, and enthralling with your talks,
moments, and meetings that,
my mind was only on you,
nothing outside was...
anything in front of you.
Thus, being never worked on myself-keeping or skills,
and thus publicly, haplessly I lost you.
Thus, in human society rather than pea-size brained of Peacocks,
dreaded every moment of this kind but,
rather than a continuation of you,
thus, what I got was enough of you.

What The Aspect Seems

I have a strength of character,
I have a grit,
which despaired too much...
now it's high time,
you are not so eligible!!
Will turn into two cappuccinos,
on the table, closer enough,
to break the possible deal, I know.

Lost and depressed,
what people or that particular person would think!!
Now changing the city, I changed people,
no one knows my history,
a stalwart future has to come,
now met with more dominant men with more domain,
whatever boss he was in my past thinking,
he has nowhere to stand or come,
even myself, after achieving a bit too... too big,
and grit even more,
now the superlative thing, I am myself,
not dominating or dominant and likely for no purpose of
intimidating, but...
I am a self-influencer.
What the aspect seemed,
that was not the actual aspect pertaining is confirmed.
Thus,
Even the thought of being so much thought person or past influencer,
is not coming or has to come,

not biased, but suppose...
I met PM Modi (shook hands),
why would I be registering MLAs???
like if I climbed Mount Everest,
then my mind would register acme,
the pinnacle of the Mount Everest,
and would elapse time obsessively thinking of it,
what to think about small step hills?
even (specifically or in general),
I am lower than an achieved MLA, then too generally that comes,
I am greatest,
and the difference is much more,
in the coming company and curriculum.
Eye contact was not my prodigy ever,
like an ostrich on a big thing, whatever to save the eggs,
gazes down, heads down, submissive...
now habitual eye contact is the instinct developed due to achievement and achievements of mine,
now enthralling, captivating others, with my confidence is my self-hypnosis,
averse to my former behaviour,
in a stagnant state, avid, inclined,
unique, mesmerizing,
now I am not a pendulum...
by default, everywhere showcasing,
point A to point B where ever I have to go,
whatever I have to say,
I go and I blurt,
with no hesitation.
It feels good to great,
that —
I am not a request,
I am the ultimatum.

When No Caffeine

I read science and questioned:
to excel the human race, can't science evolve...
and come up with a formula with no sleep to program humankind?
even more breaking the barrier, and performance it can do!

Like especially my concern for me,
if I am capable of reading 60 pages in 60 minutes,
if time is thirty minutes... 30 pages is a loss for me,
due to my family requiring or whatever.
Now, what to do??
Is there any incantation even for my personal preference?
so that, I may take the workload even more to be the greatest,
rather than blank and numb replaced by lively moments of hue,
or like ants do, in twelve hours only eight minutes of sleep and thus recovery,
asked the same name, Vishal IIT Bombay Professor sir too.

Because,
in the manager's important meeting, I am sleeping!
I am with this attitude disturbing, distracting others, and annoying.
Say 200 mg to 300 mg is the permissible limit of caffeine,
800-1000 mg I am introducing each day to myself and inducing...
then too, no one morally or minimally knows what I want from life,
with less than five hours of sleep, I am adapted to,
but due to whole day rest left lively living or keeping myself awake,
is like a workout, now it's a backfire too...
maximum strenuous efforts effective,
each second was perceiving, receiving, imbibing, pertaining, propelling,
enticing, believing, loading and thus, etc., etc., in making.

Then that was fatigue progression and progressing which was intolerable,
 for the fresh, eight hours, slept proper and properly managed brains of you.

I have no sloppy attitude,
hardware and software inculcate the slogan of hard work-hard work,
without showing to tread you,
without expecting any compensation from you,
or margin of condition applied:
you saying "understanding."
I just want to say,
I am the father of you,
and,
yes, with this loss of control turned prominent lethargy,
one day, nothing personal, but this kicked brain from classrooms with no interest in the curriculum of subjects,
will achieve much more than you.
When no caffeine,
there is my inbuilt 'adrenaline rush' from the glands over the kidney for you.

I will snatch everything over my capacity, present decently,
best selective process,
believe me!!
in the near future, soon...
with my trembling hands too.

1403 Kilometre Distance

1403 km difference!!
now cities are different but,
before, in the same city, many times...
she sat on the pillion i.e., on the back seat of my — the same bike,
parcelled from my former city by train to Mumbai.

Today I imagined suddenly,
in her absence,
between our elated talks, a sudden disturbance!
she is taking the phone from her black jeans' back pocket,
and picking up a call from my mother-in-law.

"*Haan maa sab badhia theek hai yha...
wo... bike chala rhe hai*" then the whole conversation...
(we are married).

Like at random,
just a moment felt and gone,
which was supreme divine.

I Being A Poet, You Helped Me, In Many Poems Of Mine

I plunged and dived into deep water,
to crave each second more and more,
much more for life,
being a poet, you helped me,
in many poems of mine.
I have just and just...
Girl described, elaborated, and displayed you like...

Whenever you go through your existential crisis,
whenever you are unable to link confirmed confidence with you,
whenever you lose yourself,
even you to yourself...
original versus you, whatever is described,
just come to the written pieces and poems of mine...
and see how many aspects, and perspectives you have,
and what you are at a point in time,
even this time,
has nothing to do with;
love, affection, and feelings of mine.

You are again giving me a new whole story of you.
I will convert that too... into a beautiful rhyme,
your cantankerous things are too...
for the later versions of you to laugh in the tunes of time,
and Girl, without saying, I Love You!!
Will you marry me (directly)???
you will come to know,
I am nothing,

my whole life scenario is your whole life scenario,
dedication, perseverance, reverence, trust, support, etc., etc., and, of course, whatever is in and outside these all combined,
in and at each word which made sentence,
for forever and ever and ever like;
I am saying... in my journals,
nocturnal and diurnal and in between any word which is still not found,
or described by humans,
to describe the adventures of us to aeon.

Will you be mine...????

Hollywood

Like oxen for ploughing,
Pitbull, bloodhound the bravest, not Pomeranian or something.

195 countries,
in numerous divided, and subdivided...
cast, creed, and breeds.

This time, the bravest is me, a Bengali,
I will not back down.
Will kill myself in achieving,
not Bollywood...
Hollywood— I am coming.

An instinct of madness is necessary,
was quilting,
now expanding.

My 1st book, " Ma Aksar Likhta Nahi"
Released on October 2020

Shahrukh Khan sir signed copy and wrote
"To, Vishal, lots of love and happiness"
On 11-February-2025

Every Bit Connotes Me To You

I am enjoying,
there is nothing alike,
my degradation is happening...
by the thoughts of you.

My instincts confirm,
my major time, for which I should be an avid,
best should be seeing the ceiling,
myself in the position of being supine,
with two hands folded below my pensive head and legs crossed,
you are my Netflix, Cartoon Network, Amazon Prime.
Sometimes behind the shades, sparkling eyes...
in public, in my reminiscent mood,
then too... forget about my glees, in sorrows too, I feel divine.

Actually, factually, and eventually!!
every bit connotes me to the supreme,
my mind goes not to adjacent,
but goes to and demands superior,
whatever you do is an unbeatable, inimitable class of you,
forget about you... how much!
Even, every pretty girl turns me into you.
Actually, a struggling girl too...
I go to you... I remember you,
a boy has nothing alike.

Factually, eventually, the best essence...
the best musk scent that smells feminine is you,
nothing to loiter upon,

like all they are partials and thus instigate and give direction to you,
like on a bus, someone on the seat has a dream of Mercedes too.

I am known,
even being like a celebrity treated by many,
nothing in front of you,
being SRK your favourite,
you are a die-hard fan,
were you? Or are you able to divert five minutes of his attention on you???
or even two minutes???
or even ever have had a glance of him on you???
so just think, my life is so blessed!
I talk to you daily...
being an artist, you too a dancer, I am your biggest fan,
you are my SRK.
I can't believe it many times,
I am so capable of having minutes and add-ons of you.
I talk to you daily,
literally, I thank God daily for the grace of you.

Literally, I thank God daily for the grace of you,
being a trainer, nutritionist, and yoga instructor officially and by allowing care of you, by you too... unofficially too,
solving you daily,
your pain, discomforts, misery, and bad day by themselves because of me a bit,
eliminating their form on you.
By this,
giving you and your thoughts agility,
loving myself even more,
that for you, I am worthy,
and thus, getting more than friendly behaviour from you.

My heart claiming,
hopes and expectations all would become reality,
gradually, eventually by...
whatever the paved roads I am getting to perform for the well-being and betterment of you.
Being a health coach,
immense education thus with a brilliant mind!
Not like relationships, "*Mere babu ne khana khaya,*"
but being your nutritionist for a lifetime, even...
how to, what to eat, protein, fat and carb, in what proportion and quality, quantity, combination teaching you is much greater,
than just - "*Mere bubu ne khana khaya?*"
concern for you.
My study of nutrition science is successful by this only, nothing much more fillip giving substance more than in front of my eyes, the well-being of you,
and me myself thanking you,
that maximum time I'm with my favourite person, is better than yesterday, i.e., you.
As the story proceeds and culminates from the unknown us,
in this aspect or by this aspect,
I am much more ethically important, and I am a support system for you.
Forgetting about my food and nutrition, even being a food science expert and nutritionist!
I am mesmerized as a die-hard fan and admirer of you... when I am not getting you, I just rewind you,
it's an aviation without plane, by the thoughts of you.
We are very close talking every day, not today!
But it is much more important getting closer each day...
by the proceedings of you and combined reliance to obvious us,
I Love you.
Will you marry me???

I am healthy, skilful, looking good, decent, and now have money, Girl,
and from way long, belonging to a good family,
would you mind???
If I would ask...
I am willing to take my life's biggest decision with you???

She Is An Addiction Undefined

I am always on the spin with much more effort...
of my mental engine.

The container is not much enough to contain...
tears in my eyes,
are the spills of built-up extra moments and time.

Like a jot of curd,
makes a liquid milk,
changes the character,
into semi-solid, solid...
same, her one thought!
cuts the outside world and whatever the related other than love
rhymes.
I know...
I know what to leave and for my consciousness on what to thrive...
but she is an addiction undefined.
I am blessed!!
The dream was to touch the sky, but...
that a jot or whatever of that very dreamed girl I got,
whenever she gave the proximity,
I am a lot different.
Every moment with her...
was a cloud nine.

Due to her immensely...
I am not bored with myself at all.
Even whoever, wherever with whatever circumstances and occurrences
I am in,

I am always in sync with those unforgettable times...
to intrigue her ever for longer duration of talks, was my achievement,
I was a heroic thing internally in myself summarized.

A Nincompoop

A Nincompoop, silly, nerd got you for whatever time,
in Hindi, there is a saying "*Langoor k hath me angoor.*"
Or,
my talent and status, possible position attracted you,
you are mean or your grace or with no option,
or me having just something to adore or incline.
Whatever the perspective!!
doesn't matter, Girl!!
only this jot in a plethora of whole lot matters,
I got you for myself, whatever with the mutual we have, Girl...
with perfect probability, and with proper perfect tunes of time.
That probability is too after zero point (0.) then zero then...
following numerous infinite 0...0...0...
and then indeed a crucial 1.
Until and unless even the second lively planet would be discovered,
whatever... for the average to get better or to suffice,
but...
Sun has gravitational force with perfection so, thus Earth revolves around,
or earth has a purpose to overcome minus immense degree of only death enthralling clime!
Science, evolution, or Shiva, Vishnu, Brahma.
Whatever, whoever!!
It's too the last topic for probing,
so, leave this topic related too behind,
but no audacity maximum of questioning,
I am alive, that matters most and utmost,
I am living blessed, that's it.

Indeed, in the laboratory and in the bunch of all chemicals,
homogeneous and heterogeneous things,
if I am substance and you are substance,
from one nook I was picked up, you from another corner,
at least we are interacting,
like proper flow and phonetics of a rhyme.
A person like you...
belongs to me, it's the thing.
With dark bold letters prominently prominent even... from the rest,
at the most important page,
of an important only known book like...
then too underlined.

Brahmos Missile

I wish to give her only soothing moments.
She doesn't love me, then too,
her life should be simplified by me.
I will be there always,
for that strong enough woman,
whatever will come to her,
to gauge my strongness, the toughness of mine.
I love her internally in tears very much,
whenever I interviewed myself many times,
don't know when from normal it happened!
I am a devotee, and she is divine.
She is somewhere else!
I said to her, "you have a Brahmos Missile at Mumbai."
From any boy, don't be cringed, don't be afraid,
whatever the case, it matters,
I am always there for you,
just trigger the target,
she smiled with the cutest smile.

From timid, like cowed always,
now what she inscribed and carved!!
An Alpha male without a wine,
that confirmed confidence in myself to do anything for her is the takeaway high,
that was the from a long time,
searched bravery of mine,
whatever turns she may go...
but she is like a self-purpose, motive-defined.

She is inside me, more than myself to get the tenacity for...
to do anything list.
I am blessed by a swollen manly chest,
that no perceived examples by eyes, felt phrases or flimsy hero,
gave on time.

Conscious Efforts For You, Too Much Girl

Countenance,
Or whatever the circumstances I would be,
words, manipulation, accent, temper control, tones, even break with
even commas in the sentence,
to spell in a sense,
all measured and all would be measured.
Even suppose two nights after suffering, no sleep, or for four nights...
I am sleep-deprived,
the seizures if, then too!
I may not care about anyone, but...
decency will be utmost followed, no doubt for you selflessly,
conscious efforts for you,
too much, Girl!!
You are strong, but,
you are a fragile thing in me,
too much... intermediately.
Even forget about yourself sitting sadly!!
resist even clicking...
showing artistic majesty,
on your Facebook, Instagram, posts and stories,
with a mourning face, gazes down,
a woollen bear/teddy bear,
to add on, with a sad induced by a music theme in the background,
making it even more gloomy!
Rather than click some flying pigeons,
or like,
nut-relishing squirrels in a garden,
wholeheartedly.

Your inclination...
even disturbs me!
Turns me pesky.
I turn into a different person... next very second when perceived,
believe me...
you can't track yourself to those,
even a bit of those recordings may not feel soothing as it is different in your subconscious...
subconsciously,
but in the aspect of life, it connotes sad emotions distinctly,
and capturing those aspect is too an artistic majesty,
but,
without any propulsion or imposed on to feel,
giving me a clear different clime, uneasy too inadvertently.
Please have some empathy,
as I am interconnected to you from my side immensely,
on me have some mercy.

Your Inclinations, Even Disturbs Me

I am a two-body person.
Be happy, always for me,
up to whatever extent you can...
after that, please allow me.

Don't show me,
what you observe, Girl,
especially your sadness,
how much I am selfless for you,
I came to know,
even in front – whatever the important time,
in which I should be.

A person is an individual "I,"
is known to the trauma of his for long.
I am okay.
I am negligent with mine.
But...
you with your camera... the saddest act or portrait,
on your Instagram Story,
a Teddy bear even with a slouch back seems sad and in sorrow,
can't get much deeper,
even being artificial,
it will break my heart,
and will sparkle tears in my eyes.
Why do you capture that?
why your inclinations are so such like?

whatever the important work I have,
my mind would be diverted in a single second even many times.
You are not allowed,
when to me you are so vibrant, lively, and divine.

I can't say,
even being awesome,
even that artistic touch nice.
Thus,
for more closer to genuine and awesome pieces,
I can't entice.

Vishal Sarkar,
The Best For You For Lifetime

Every time you slipped like...
seemed it was a deprivation from you of a lifetime.
Way back and even recently,
count it, Girl, it happened many times.

I went under the great depression,
recovered and thanked,
for whatever even seconds, we added mutual,
and enjoyed like...
closed eyes never felt anything,
but open eyes with dilated pupils,
have seen only ecstasy, charms, mirth, and beauty of this only life.

And falling in love with you,
there again forgetting the pain of depart...
and disheartening of mine.
Many, and many times,
I have given every test and trial of true love,
even after losing you, I was...
loving you like a child of mine.
A strong man needs to hold the woman tightly as if in one unit.
Now through the process,
undeterred from anyone,
even deterrent to others I am,
if you are there or on the other side...
that's the cost same to my life.
Raise the bar; I will slay the gauge every time.
Now from good, better, best to a superlative degree man, I am,

to cope with the insecurities of the unanimous cacophony of...
 how come???
for those only...
to get the greatest price of you,
I became a tank in front of guns.
Now marry me.
Description: I will not tell of mine,
but,
your surroundings too, with no doubt or question marks, would say...
Vishal Sarkar!!
the best for you, for a lifetime.

She Gives Me Mental Stability

A favourite girl and best friend of mine from my side,
shares her every schedule of work, headache, stomach cramps to joint
pains, anxiety, sulk, depression, mood swings, temper.
Averse reverse behaviour,
due to somewhere instigated by others at work, workplace, home, or
community.
Cantankerous even due to those even on me (the repercussions),
as somewhere she knows simply, she is my lady.

That's how my life feels easy,
due to a working lady.
Being the hardest worker in the hemisphere or room,
whenever I feel my body the same or trembling,
I am feeble due to the overexert,
due to less than usual sleep and aggregation of going brutal, due to
work and work on me...
to be the cream.
Joint pain, muscle pain, spasm, or headache, even before having balm
or thinking,
I just feel the girl whom I love.
An adhesiveness comes thus more in understanding her,
she gives thus the direction,
diversion from me,
she must have felt the same as a working lady,
says my instincts.
What I feel or felt is not new,
she also feels the same,
there is no speciality.
If a girl power can resist,

what about a so-called masculinity?

Thus, I love her,
even more...
I am not only,
if a cutie pie, can bear!
come give me much more quota...
for my manly macho behaviour.
Whatever body, mental, or even instability,
following her, remembering her, reciting her,
even is a catharsis.
She gives me mental stability,
to withstand the opposite of common and to fight the dreaded,
it's too unknown a very soothing talent of my bestest bestie.

Tunes Of Time

In spite of having good skin, proper hygiene, a delicious face, brawn strength, and intelligence quotient (IQ) too...
I don't believe in hard work.
Thus,
I believe in luck.

See...
I love you blindly, totally.
No one can love you more than me, Girl.
My hopes diminish entirely,
from demolished those,
I have hopes again...
wholeheartedly.

People by others' phrases...
"Ghalib's shers" make crush, their girls!!
Even with piracy, no originality from beginning to just fallacy.
And see...
I wrote 811 approximately poems with my mind, heart, and soul,
for you, on you... each taking 5-5 hours of work,
811 × 5 = 4055 hours, approximately,
from when we are in touch and contact just generally.
More than this –
going to publish a book with inscribed all the care but no flaunt or showcasing,
"Tunes of Time... Incessant You,"
with maximum you.

I am still trying hard,
then too struggling,
and...
and like I am still enjoying the probability,
my case is still pending...
like in the immediate imminent times no relation with you,
just totally losing.

If There Are No Add-Ons

You will not be continuing with me.
So, what!!
if I was to die,
probably –
there was not going to be any add-ons of you.

I am alive!!
Thus,
I will with my mind, psychology, conscience, imagination,
will fill the pages of time.
Will make many shades, and copies, with nuances, layers, contrast,
brightness, colours, etc.,
of the perceived and observed original you.

I had big dreams for this lifetime,
to have you, but then too...
for every extensive hope, expectation, and demand internally,
for every no versus...
a bit whatever more to satisfy my craving I got,
by heart, thank you.

Places have energy,
people have too...
the minimum was too uncontrollable!
with chain reactions like radioactive atoms, maximum of you.
Honestly, I am so blessed to have been through whatever confronts
possible,
and made many sentences,
with you in conversations.

I got like a fan moment with a celebrity revered like you,
whether I may say you sweetheart or not,
to... beloved or myself your beau or not.

Let everything go averse of the feeling of loving you.
Let's then too... let me,
love you.

I Am Gandhi

I love her immensely, amazingly, without any doubt, but...
it's the immensely immense possessiveness of me,
and I am working on this character of mine.

Being in another city far from her,
when I see her on Instagram, or somewhere...
a guy becoming cosy and much more to her!
comments like more than normal more!
or when she is talking to another guy!
I too became talkative with some of my office girls...
or to whom so good never got the chance to talk flawlessly,
due to the reserved character of mine.
Exceeding, only Hii... Hello even to the new ones many times,
breaking not the limits,
but to quench like to nullify being in another city.
Thus, that much-believing character is dented too of mine...
I love her like with no distractions,
at the middle single point black,
dart hit like.
It's crazy, but I am one of a kind.

I manage how talkative in the utmost limits, ambits of...
where there is the other side of my, is a flirt or a pick-up line,
and the centre was in me a shy guy,
without crossing the circular motion...
a stone tied with a thin rope revolves like.

It's crazy, it's psycho!!
It happens internally in me just one or two times.

Not to show her tit for tat, but...
but every next second later,
It becomes an equalizer.
With this agenda,
the grace of well-being becomes the skin of mine,
for a grudge-free healthy heart, the next second becomes the well-being of mine.

I am Gandhi :).
Like... sorry the essence of Gandhi,
70-80 years ago...
just as a mother, very vexed with his child's jaggery eating habit,
seeking help from M.K. Gandhi.
In between four weeks, Gandhi returns lady with just elapsing time with her problem.
Last time in the fourth week, when he said to the child decently,
"*Beta!!* don't eat a lot of what you are eating, jaggery!
Everything more than enough is fatal and unhealthy."
Only with these magical words when his mother asked Gandhi,
"Why didn't you tell these simple sentences before?"

He said a lot of jaggery eating is too binge eating habit of mine,
I was too trying to get rid of this habit,
I was curtailing in between meanwhile.
What I preach should be the practice of mine.

So, as Gandhi did it became an equalizer.
Me too doing to detect and point out the weak points without spat or arguing with her,
by behaving like her,
the same with others to normalize.

M.K. Gandhi came to the child's level,
thus, with her, with my beliefs, the limit of hangouts,
I too match my level of mine with her,
myself to pacify.

Grief's Optimum Auto-Correction

Truth is the brunt...
and I am such a case.
I may go broke anytime...
don't know up to what time!
she is in conversation,
still, it's my fortune...
due to that beautiful girl,
I am so fortunate.
Love!! Thank you for choosing me...
with her, so coincidences and so compassion,
not like once in a blue moon,
in the whole lifetime.

Probability, pain, grace —
everything is in her.
How much is the time left; I don't know!!
but I want to elapse more and more,
being in continuation of being lucky,
rather -
being helpless, unlucky, weeping.
(Knowing the truth).
As I have nothing to engage other than her,
in the upcoming too tide of time,
tears shall come as much as late,
as much euphoric illusion,
as much late time could bring.
No stay is an already guarantee of her,
let her go...

missing her would be...
my loving, lovely passion,
like to my restless mind the sound of soothing chimes,
and I will wholeheartedly follow...
I have already felt the intuitions,
whatever I got is enough!!
What was I???
If even that was not???
Is my, what life has done to me?
Question's!
"Grief's Optimum Autocorrection,"
like brief but comprehensively gist concise.
After her -
I know, in many and many reputations, I would be a human
ragpicker... madly devouring onto dine,
very calm even with immovable eyeballs,
paralyzing all my actions...
I become, when into my mind she comes...
she increases in coming with elapsed time,
body needs full concentration...
every other thing is untrue,
so,
nothing should cross or should instigate any conversation or argue.
With my hands crossed, folded like "do not disturb,"
and hijacked conscience,
without inebriation of wine...
it's most external or internal, I don't know,
but with her, cutting all,
I am in a silent, loquacious drive.

Bosses!! See Thus I Will Backfire

Whenever life put me,
to learn lessons or give me open wounds or open lesions,
I optimally, according to my cognition,
how much the level I had,
I grabbed it, with the lesson,
did it positive...
and too, rest missed it.

I have seen myself in trouble,
being redundant and amateur,
and superlative persons or bosses like...
wholeheartedly teaching many and many times,
or exaggerating once in a blue moon, and seldom like brutally barking at me,
and levelling all the previous good and makeup, patching up matters,
and if it happens, assuming me frail frequently,
see, thus, I will backfire.
Whatever I am in expertise with USP is...
my concentration, knack, hard work, and talent,
it's great I get lauds —
that's my strong enough point...
I will enhance it,
and will fortify myself too...
with the incurring demands,
by working on flaws of barking,
then, being superior and ideal!
will damn charge it!
"An old mamma gives blessings,"
on giving a bread or by helping her to cross the road,

that's another story and thing...
but,
money is the respect for the value.
Nothing much other than more, I think.
When I had nothing like company to give,
rhetorical regular dialogues of worthlessness,
don't be a liability to the company!!
So, I am proclaiming,
in the future, I will cost like anything.
Untalented, useless like, backbencher is nothing, but I am in the middle,
have worked for my career...
and independent good happenings.
If too...
History is tainted and dented by,
taunts of incompetence and thus incompatibility.
Future is loaded with synonyms of endeavour and praises,
point to be noted,
like Police never thrashes like the first,
not for wearing a helmet—
it's not correct ethics.
In any case, in human society first,
it charges a fine, to degrade mental sanity,
like Police have some talks,
somewhere sometimes it seems like,
just as the reverse and averse of abuses...
it's yours, when I am going well, there are praises!!
Bosses!!
No personal matter, matters especially.
Bosses!!
I don't need praise as such.
I am something if,
then give me enhanced, extended money,

because of my poor time gauges...
not much or that much of your lauds.
Your praises came way later!!
"Like you, there are many,"
to only me...
i.e. Vishal Sarkar,
I have a day in and day out,
sacrificed the greatest daily.

It was majorly the fire of incompetence and thus,
abusive nature and barking nature of yours onto me...
which remained more than embers, burning and unquenched.
Simply I have that's why,
pulled me out and outnumbered me alone,
verses other than ordinary...
from your tongue and mouth combined,
I have made these praises, accolades, and phrases,
like an eureka moment in my mind of shrine and sanctity,
in lieu of or rather than cacophony.

At this point, I am—
don't know at what thinking process I would be!!
but it's nothing...
in the future, I will cost you like anything.
I am proclaiming, acclaiming, loading skills, and assiduously wise already saying,
I am the greatest...
and with the chronological and biological ages both enhancing...
much more great,
to claim is important as a notice.

That's why openly writing is encapsulating.

You Are A Goddess To Me, In The Religion Of Love

You were a goddess to me,
in the religion of love.

Life has been so treacherous to me,
that the ground slipped every time,
whenever I relaxed, claiming,
after tussling and winning with assurance...
that it was mine.

Care, affection, security, honesty —
all I showed for you,
because for you, I had...
but you too became the same case for me.

No issues, Girl!!
but feeling pity for myself,
that your memories will in a good way, irk me.
Well, then too... I will say,
I am grateful,
when I am in tears,
each time I will feel you the most.
I will go there to meet the best person in my life whom I met... no grudges,
I will laugh at your tantrums... omitting all odds,
which were like a child's,
nocturnal, diurnal and daily.

Thanking you... too, for all the beautiful nuances, layers, flavours,
essences of including, and the indulging painful ones.
When someone flaunts their love story,
in the backseat, in a car, I will be not flaunting,
but thank you...
that's because of you,
I can feel that I fell...
and I too had a love story.

Why Not Only Me!!

Everything has pros and cons...

Pro is—
They say - "Don't get distracted,
achieve your goals."
This means - girls are distractions, means to say.
But my story is... I am a poet.
She will love me, ditch me, betray me, block me, or whatever!
I will turn that into verses.
Yaa... it's painful, not easy to say, and too not easy to elaborate,
then too,
I am so fortunate :).
Whatever she would do,
she is indeed independent, so am I.
But then too, she would with her absolutes,
indirectly is converted into pages and then into money,
throughout the day and ages.

But the con is -
I am afraid of my future wife, if she is, then ok.
otherwise!!
"From where these inspirations came before me?"
I will be bombarded,
and my whole life with her like... I will be under fallacy,
and,
with less to-be-trusted expectancy,
with pages, references, and records,
during spats and quarrels, I think!

With a sharp eye,
she will judge me...
even if I say, I wrote verses on her, then too,
in those three-four days, she will be like,
why not only me??
Rascal...!!
Who is before me... he is such a published party changer!!
My books on Amazon and Flipkart, etc., will be a shame for me,
quality writings I will not recite, as it will be as–I will be remembering her,
somewhere in the past, whom I wanted to be wholeheartedly...
life, talent, and hard work are a heck...
believe me.

With Everything, I Accept You

Come on...!!
You know like a child develops from 1+1 cell to a zygote, then
forwards to an infant,
falters, falls, and then he sometimes post...
receives, perceives, runs well, and talks better,
life and mind too... develop with time,
and with every encounter, people hone the internal matter.

In you and I, I mean in both of our lives—
there were some special,
that's why we have mature talks, behaviour,
nourished indications,
to do/not to do foresight and imagination that matter,
even sentences that we are listening to,
with phonetics,
will not subtract, like it's like the tick of time—
an adding matter.

And come on, too!!
in our 20... 30,
interaction with someone or other deep and good...
is obvious.
Otherwise, you are semi-loathed and a nerd,
I think in personality too...
you are void and null,
that's why I have,
and I accept you with your past,
with an experienced person like you...
and me,

for our harbingering future.

In a tome/book of your life,
I want to be the most filled pages, most interesting, and the last chapter.

It's Sunday Morning Then Too

It's Sunday morning,
maximum everybody is sleeping,
and recovering from the...
Monday, Tuesday, Wednesday, Thursday, Friday, Saturday all hectic.
Like 10-12 hours immersed in engaging sleep,
and see, it's me at 4:00 AM Sunday!
no weekends off,
as you are still continuing like a must-matter.

To disconnect from you... on an out-of-context matter,
I was reading a book...
two hours, I was into it,
I finished 20 pages only.
You interfered in... many times,
whatever context!!
in receiving anything, you are a greater,
so, I must muster.

Now finished, like that was a hindrance!!

Now,
I allowed you to pass throughout my mind.
come to the memories with past and in making upcoming future,
for network hindrance,
not windows or doors I have opened,
but suppose!!
with my consent, four walls have fallen,
and the roof too on a safe side.
Just imagine,

without sound, ruffle, or clutter...
now you and my mind are a receiver of the most interesting matter.

Thank you,
no need for a song, movie, Netflix, or a Cartoon Network,
like a harmless enchanted matter,
you are way... way... more... better.

Percentage Of Receiving

I was averse to conferences and meeting people,
only enjoyed my hangouts with solitudes,
since long, but... but...
now sociopathy is going from me,
by believing in the concept...
like "Baali" took half of every and became 50% more immensely
indispensable, unbeatable...
in an enmity way,
in a destructive way.
From then (listening to the ancient tales),
this belief system in me started internally inculcating...
like not a masterpiece and an expert like him,
but I don't suck for instance 1-2 %,
but inculcate, imbibe like 1-2% in a constructive way.

In a deterrent world of men,
where I even was afraid to stand with my substantial strong legs,
inspiration, instincts, and propelling my dreams,
my self-doubting motives,
like with them competing.
A girl, bare minimum like you,
exhorts only with like in a crowd walking...
a girl, bare minimum like you,
I met her standing for her dreams versus society,
and like uneven masculinity.
More than books... I got the readings,
by only perceiving...
the whole averse is changed into a good-going.
From a brave girl like you,

I got the maximum percentage of absorbed energy,
combined of 5-6 greatest masculine and inculcating.
Thanks for you, for me...
at the proper time, place on this earth, and time elapsing.
Opposite sex you are, that's why don't know but,
the pituitary, hypothalamus, prefrontal cortex everything works best by hormonal discharging.
When you are the source and I am grabbing.
It's you girl that now, I am strong enough, I am what I am,
and no masculine can overwrite me.
In the library, and at the gym both!
in myself, I am heavily building.
So that you may feel safe,
of course, I can be for another masculine's,
having eyes on you, and me intimidating,
when you are not afraid of your surroundings,
why should I be?
When high in hormones and muscle building???
Thank you for showing...
it's you that built me mostly and majorly.
You, from a female, I am receiving like maximum like an inculcation of "Baali."
The lucky mascot for me for my good coming,
and my pleasure is that,
I am still in your contact,
and I am increasing my percentage of receiving.
I am the greatest because of you I foresee,
learning must be a boring and pesky task excruciating from a book or coaching,
but you are the best source of enthralling.

Make A Proper Caret

Being a girl itself is a catastrophe!
Understood, you are misunderstood...
that's why, in rage...
self-esteem I have tossed, like...
you are showing even what you are not to be.

Girl, I may go wrong on you,
but...
a small request with tears in my eyes – 'sorry.'
With all aversion and inversions,
will you teach me life?
Until the end of life... in company???
My masculine nature is filled with doubt,
you are great at being femininity.
Actually, I am alone half,
both two combined...
is an individual humanity.

I am not apt and good,
let's incur me with your,
flavour of life.
More nicely for my nicety then broadly,
with you and yours mixing.
Let's please make a proper caret treasury,
let's make my birth and death...
by your interference please girl,
inscribed in history.

With every walk, second, mile,
with your apt instincts please, purge me.

Experiencing Hypoventilation

Don't show me patterns and innuendos,
circumstances related... what you want to say or observing,
without telling.

I sleep less, so thus,
lack of cognition,
but I am a master at perceiving,
there too... internally I am with anxiety,
not good to carry on experiencing.
Immense assiduity or whatever showing related to whatever I am not...
even today I am experiencing,
hypoventilation (short breathing),
due to unrest, day and night—
just overthinking.

That boy has a pattern of following...
what I followed, it's distinctly ahead and seen.
It's love, affection, amour, lust, or whatever!
not ordinary I have foreseen.
Like ambits gradually,
he is gradually trespassing.

I will fall every time, when I will see you hazy or in trouble,
it's my duty and instinct,
but please do understand...
to show me!!
Okay, I am important,
you are, I swear, much more in me,
but don't let it be...

not socially that much,
now after following you on Instagram!!
On your posts he's commenting!!
and internally, with his audacity, he is increasing.

My process, and profile may be sloppy and sleepy,
no impulse reactions certainly,
but please do understand...
three decades you have elapsed on this earth,
even I matured under you,
and you are not a bimbette...
acknowledge, inform, or restrict him,
it's clear...
in hide of innocuous nicety with accumulated layers of decency,
he is chasing.

Verge Of Imminent End

There is nothing important in being weak.
You will deteriorate internally,
when the destitute creeps in...
by default, when you have no class,
what to feed or better to greed...
medium to maximum chances of being, if too down,
drunkard habitually —
for time to pass under this developed instinct.

Crossing this—
in the middle, like good,
the crowd is good and you can conclude yourself as a thing.
But still, you are...
tested and perceived that 24 hours are less for survival instincts.
Miscellaneous misconceptions, unsatisfied behaviour, cantankerous,
quarrelsome cries are frequent everywhere.
Like from the totally dependent infant, adolescent to maturity, the size
is increasing.
Here, if probed, life is like a live autopsy.

Then crossing this—
now challenges are bigger than you,
no matter who you are,
there comes being superlative...
superlative degree men!
detrimental, mature with more equipped weapons;
like you for achievement, generally, they have more conceit.
They are allied or foes, watch it.

In between whatever...
the rest is "all roads... will tell the theory."
Before the verge of the imminent end,
everything is life's lively activities...
acknowledge it... bigger or smaller everywhere is a live autopsy,
and,
everyone whoever the rest is a good Samaritan, that's why they will say...
worship God,
make a place for him in your heart.
Only then this hectic will be less incurring...
the place will become far from worthless to worth living.

I Am A Beautiful Person In All Syncs, Though Will Improve The Average

I was just enormously influenced by my emotional heart's mincing,
from my sudden, relied on broken existence.

A stance, a word, a sentence, a behavioural outcome, a retort,
doesn't mean that's why...
that much anything, even more at a glance.

I didn't elaborate my heart and his full content,
that doesn't mean I was full of that only...
to intimidate you or to show my area and my dominance.

I am a beautiful person in all syncs,
though will improve the average,
will apply what I feel then too...
what should I reflect,
with age and time much more elegantly distant.

Like a car without a proper driver,
might go awry,
that's not the car itself.
Yes, I know!
I am at a loss of emotional intelligence,
otherwise no drama or impure heart,
for the brethren...
only bonhomie is the unlimited,
without a boundary and circumference,
and so and so...
whatever you will reciprocate,

far and furthermore,
now will be neglected, even in the aggregated interests,
someone may take it as compensation, but there will be tolerance.

My Girl Is Going

I am going to lose my second love and beloved in life.
In "married to someone else" tragedy.
I think now again this time respectively,
due to my incompetency.

It's an alarming situation,
told herself too...
that a beautiful thing like love,
after you,
I will do it a third time too.
Most experienced, with life and time,
much more brutally thrashed,
wholeheartedly,
will not even beat next time!!
but will beat with a distant distance certainly.
Beware, more the masculine's,
from any Tom, Dick, and Harry with competency, I will be a
personality.
For instance—
if behind a kite,
there are two, three, or more many,
I will better know,
she is not a kite 🪁 actually...
and that's the best selective process.
Yeah, there the future Tom, Dick, and Harry!!
you are an adolescent maybe!
but I am more expert, and experienced with lessons and lesions,

actually, factually, and eventually,
there is no form more than the worst,
but I am even worse...
if next time,
a low-experienced in one shot, wannabe wins,
with fewer sessions and seasons of his life.

Rationally, in a good way,
It's now my self-esteem.
Third love, I am coming,
whatever the stages are shameless again, let it be,
yes, yeah, the same or more than amorous I would be.

I will take revenge for my mediocrity,
unable to interact with men.
I will kill the talented masculinity,
by my talented audacity.
The best selective process already said...
with status,
other than this, in a good way,
what could it be?
more thrashed by kismet,
more potency,
how to remove the dents of past encounters being older,
it would be my prodigy.

Girl... Girl...
I am just joking,
Girl... just an ordinary sentence but... but...
no one can love you like me.
If you want to come back,
please choose to marry me,
we will live hereafter happily.

I came from "Hindi Shairy" to English,
to curtail the crowd which understands linked meanings,
with an agenda to conceal,
then too... each word is like connoting you,
and sentences are not an alibi.

I am not here to resemble myself,
as a stud one, two, three...
I love you still actually,
unconscious and consciously
unconditionally.

Don't Bewitch Your Surroundings

Not every time sharing,
or it's worth sharing.

The tragedy is!!
when someone is shaken, quaked internally,
despair, and sudden storm,
claims its place like a gush internally.

They need a personal space and time,
to settle, to reset, to magnify,
the former form or instinct,
not immediately but gradually.

But they are in public,
with people around,
and they make mistakes by interacting,
where there was a need for solitude and resting...
creeps in!!
Use of words without thinking abruptly,
body language is worse than neglecting,
whose examples are never settling.
Note: Many times, people too never show tacit understanding,
that's why it's better,
don't be a celebrity,
don't bewitch your surroundings.

It's Not People's Fault Actually

It's not people's fault actually.
While seeing some pitiful minds,
I observed totally that...
I was too the same culprit of instincts.

How much!
I have done hard work,
to achieve the present conscience,
it's commendable.
Thus -
I feel for myself proud too,
as I am distinct.

Feminism

Rascals will think of bed and bed!
Covertly, overtly!
only as an instinct,
I know.

Just for an instance,
Feminism can be weak,
but a so-called weak girl or woman,
working and fighting for bread and butter,
in this male-dominant world...
can give you inspiration,
and may improve your instinct and to do better,
like no man can.

Remember that...
more the minimum, more the clap for her...
one or two in a bus early morning and while returning late,
is not an opportunity...
it's a phenomenon of tenacity still,
and not dwindling.

Thank You2

I fall in love genuinely with myself, Girl.

Seeing in what condition and conditions,
I am loving you.
Initially, I was a fan of yours,
a stalker on Instagram.

Never thought!!
from fumbles in front of you,
I would be able to say,
I love you.

The allowance of proximity,
and in between instances are enough.

Thank you, for the path,
and on it,
from you, all the literacy.

But from now on,
from alphabets A to C or D or E,
I am no longer in the race,
I am no more in the efforts of interchanging myself,
as per the efforts of myself versus the others for you certainly.

It's A Human Psyche

It seemed to me, she too came to know slightly,
that I was interested in her.

It's a stage thing,
I recited my poem,
she totally comprehended, probed must be,
by emotion, inspiration, and feelings...
I am not untouched!
In my oration, a person seemed,
"Code of Conduct."

She came, recited hers with more descriptions,
about a boy in her life's voyage,
with seemed tactful, taunting, laid-emphasis.
Then what??
total cessation of every occurring emotion,
both two poet and poetess— me and she — went home of theirs,
with no matter to adjust!!

It's a human psychology and human chronology too... thus,
the insight of feelings commencing and about to commence
disappeared,
with never said!!
Rascal...
how someone is related to you that much???

Past love becomes love's alive postmortem,
so, never be so overt, brave heart.
With all the algorithms,

otherwise, rather than in the making, it would be...
beautiful future's autopsy,
it's a human psyche.

I Am The Greatest

Yes, it's positivity and success.
I am on a slant of most probably...
easy downhill now.
Uphill excruciating feeling climbers,
coming from sucking foothills, watch your steps,
take me as an inspiration, no jealousy.
If jealousy—
It will distress you and distract you,
with sudden turns and more indifference.

Now read this again,
and take it seriously,
rather meanwhile, I hope inadvertently,
don't lose the instinct of me.
Tore ligaments and many neurons, like internally bled and blended!
I have gone through all the atrocities!
Through delicacy versus audacity,
that's why I feel life and winning so sufficiently, adequately, and
succinctly.

As usual,
all I have paid the price, as the legends say.
Rather still don't know whether coming is still decent or prejudice,
it's all the world... whole is a labyrinth meanwhile many times,
a little smile then the imminent catastrophe.

Life is so averse, reverse, unfair, unexpected,
that on a black tarred road,
with me on bike at over medium speed,

mind supposes a black shawl fallen,
due to not being tied up properly by some lady,
with her stud hubby,
internally, while thinking it was a black puppy,
I just manoeuvred so hastily, wrongly,
that the unimaginable happened, everything gone!!

And at the same point in sync everything out of the kismet legacy,
due to pity.

Anger! Many A Time Leads To Bravery And Many A Times It Drains Like The Internals

Fearlessness for whatever reasons!!
Hormones Testosterone, Adrenaline, and so on...
gives these frequent surges,
being exposed to regular induced stimulations,
fighters, have this mode more...
for some reasons,
from flight to fight!!
they have the sensitivity switch,
with practice, it activates with some twitch or fewer conditions.

Sword is in the sheath,
I am a high-tempered person.
In day-to-day tussle,
I quench it by writing rhymes,
it's not to boast like...
it drains like the internals,
and may have serious repercussions.
But, with anger comes,
the "High" of let it be,
or "Come what may,"
sudden—
alienation from the love of being alive.

Yes, anger is powerful.
The dreadful becomes none of our business,
no other form of emotion,

except for some exceptions like,
mother in some catastrophe to her child.
Meanwhile, having said that,
observing love, compassion, and empathy,
many times,
may give the same selfless fly...
it's too a conclusion derived.

Otherwise laid off and calmness,
leisure, life, and being alive are divine...
rather than ruthless blood on the ground due to a gory battle, to howls in the air!
or even a dot of injection's prick,
it is always better to see the beautiful sunset and sunshine,
on anything cosily reclined.

You Are An Active And Dormant Cutie

You are an active and dormant cutie,
at the same time,
you will be.

How to harness energy,
then apply that in me against you,
I don't know.

Yes, it's not intended too...
I got my mental coordination and paths in my life due to you.
With only listening to you, your voice and words were and are
remaining, and will be the remedy,
so, what you are... or you may go awry!

For your modulation in voice,
medium to high... for whatever reasons,
I promise...
I will maintain a low pitch for you,
a respectful thing will always be respectively respectful to me.

I can't give my father my shoes to polish, no matter how much is to-go-emergency!!
for a searing rissole (samosa),
I will singe or burn my palms and hands,
if not any paper or newspaper or plate,
but will not land that,
on a paper of notebook tore on which...
I write poems or poetry!!

Non-biological things are too given respect for instances, thus no audacity.

You are a goddess to me in the religion of love.
You will give me tears then too...
I love you, damn it!!
In every demeaning, I will find a decent way for my joy to continue, unconditionally, I love you!!
then too with a hope,
that the former you,
will turn onto me.

You Are Still Present Nearby With A Chance And Probablity In My Life

Storms have come that much related to you by you.
That you will go, and will go...
but you are still present nearby with a chance and probability in my life,
as for me, you will be...

It has been years,
in between,
that top-soil is eroded totally and I am left with the base of rocks that are unable to uplift themselves,
with that minuscule amount of catastrophe,
of mental attacks that your giveaway by your father can incur on me.
Now it has become a practice, Girl.
I love you... I love you still but, thus...
thank you, nothing much painful your detachment can offer to me.
I love you still, madly, badly but rocks define here in this poem resilient and
up to a bit to maximum no effects on me,
I would say marry me but you have become that case to me!
And yes, sorry... top-soil eroded defines here,
"So many hopes shattered layer by layer and hopeless me."
Storm means your character in my life...
"With all hopes were given then snatched from me."
While taking an impromptu picture at Mumbai Beach and thinking of the recurring you,
these all verses came to me...
It's 23rd-January-2023, Sunday, 4:50 am in the morning,
thinking of you still, there are no weekends of me.

You Are A Catharsis

Many times,
when I go at those mood swings,
cantankerous, belligerent, pesky, and sulk-ridden cuss to someone...
or majorly I singe me, myself with anger to myself.
Somewhere in life or behind closed doors,
the person who comes into me, to my mind...
or comes to my rescue, is you.
I don't know, how come!!
I think with all thoughts derived that something must be,
the same happened to you at your home, work, office, or schedule.
That's why,
a few days back, you became that to me,
like the minimal percentage possible,
like without any reasonable reason to me,
you were badly connected to me.

I think that phase like (another me) crucial, came into me to understand you,
being in your shoes becomes easier for me.
To tell me and feel the same to resolve you,
more to support you, love as afore,
as the afore drive and dignity...
and Girl, it's a catharsis, believe me,
the empathy related to you comes and suddenly becomes a boon by diverting,
I love you beyond myself and all my concerns...
it's internal hooting,
never so loudly heard by any other matter close or distinct,
nothing in you then too...

if I was unable to understand you in your weak times,
and reciprocated you on your terms and conditions...
please vindicate me.

Lost work-life balance or whatever,
as an only special person to me,
I am and I will be.
With my actions and talks,
I avow,
from now, I am going to give you comfort and soothe your feelings,
that's my awesome liability,
It's the job of me.
As said —
Like first you then me, as from my side I am interconnected to you,
what happens to you, post happens to me.
Don't ever try to hide day-to-day struggles,
in your downtimes,
I am always there for you...
give that pleasure to me,
when you become gloomy,
then like you (inherited from you),
a chirping me becomes a silent me...
on a sofa or bed still and sedentary.

Rather

No hermitage needed to run from these mundane chores,
rather too...
not intended for popularity, actually afraid of!!
As it will take away my time with the most precious person alive –
that's me,
but...
I will enhance my properties and capabilities so well,
that no one will possibly,
engulf the possible possibility.

That for me it was by chance,
I was a mediocrity.

Global Patriot

Sun was born 4.5 billion years ago!
In about 6.5 billion years, it will run out of its 91% hydrogen (fuel) and will engulf,
by expanding... Mercury, Venus, and most probably the Earth.
(If not, then too... the exponential heat will evaporate all),
and then will collapse into a star known as a white dwarf!
like other stars, the same fate...
just as boiling milk expands 2-3 times like!
and spills over the brims of containers and when no energy is left to support due to cut-off of burners,
it collapses to the afore, but with some lost material,
likewise.

The above is my example because it created a reminiscent mood in me.
Actually, I have only a brother 5.5 years elder,
when I was young like 8-9 years, and he was like 14,
he used to irate and irritate me and gave me heartburn, anxiety, and sudden mood-offs by saying,
"You know, in the future Sun will be no more for us."
It irritated me very much like a depressing sudden...
(like you are saying to a feminist cute girl that women are weaker than men).
Don't know why that a lot!!
and I began to talk to him belligerently with baseless altercations...
as I didn't have the basic knowledge,
I said when I began to rationalize a bit well and good after some time with development of brain and conscience.
Once asked why so irritated, it's the truth!!

I said in a serious mood, "I think I would not be there, but the Sun should be to the Earth."

But today, going to that point...
I realize that!
that small child two decades approximately younger than the present me,
was a "global patriot."
I have not gone to the barest even minimum of the paths but after my death,
the human race should plan itineraries and should roam the unknown paths.
How inbuilt I was!
He even didn't know the sun was born 4.5 billion years ago,
will collapse totally from now about 6.5 billion years.
Then too...
what a concern it was.

Thank you :).

HAPPY AND HAPPIEST INDEPENDENCE DAY TO YOU ALL :).

I Am Running Better Than Your Brothers

I am very fortunate,
and lucky to have myself, and it's great,
that I can still take care of you.

Making a plot for the gist, but listen!!
I have only a brother 5.5 years older,
like you,
Girl!!
I have said many times (like you to your brothers) to my brother,
"I don't need any help... you moron, go to hell."
And he reverted much more the same!
and for a long time,
pact, tenacity, attitude, and determination remained the same.
Even he broke the hiatus of communication and connection broken,
he simplified himself many times,
when I came into an unsaid outside trouble!
(his helplessness).

But a long time was taken by us (both brothers),
to have an apology and for life to become easy again.

As a friend and much more from my side,
I am very fortunate...
I am a supplier of any kind of help from my side anything, anytime...
and you don't feel any extra help of mine is a proclaimed conceit of mine.
Few talks to many mutual,
even a mild association is enthralling and beautiful with you...

extended talks in any case,
it's a value exchange,
and thus, by me by you,
two lives are doing better,
with each other's concerns and...
any time's random collaborations.
Thank God!!
I haven't made any mistakes yet,
running good fortunate to say,
better than your brothers.
You haven't stopped talking to me,
from the time I know you — even once.
With your brothers just as you are belligerent enough!
but only from last some two-three years, I know you...
not like three decades in comparison but crazy average!
you are mild, I am mild,
that's insane!

By the way, Girl, just want to say,
your number of brothers three/four whatever elder,
(would not disclose this here but),
are your greatest strengths.
I know even you are feminist,
and it's too against feminism, but hold them,
don't rave about their strict behaviour,
don't break the banks.

Many times, they definitely are stalking me and my Instagram profile,
then too...
forget about other ill-minded usual boys,
I too, don't go funny beyond...
a certain level in WhatsApp or Messages.

If caught!!
and given a call???
Why to irritate them with a bit of obscene observed words or language?
all are my future relations,
all respected.
I, that's why, provide you with the simplest videos and language,
I too believe all the input on your phone determines, (uninteresting,
it's ok),
but I have gone nuts, a bit crazy or sane.

And I can bet on it!!
like my brother to me,
they will come for you to help,
without any need for accolades, or expecting any gains.

You Are A Teacher

I am too afraid of —
Whether I would be able to maintain the same energy, decorum, and cognition...
whether I will be able to entangle the front without division.
That's the thing too...
I give a maintained equivalent with not that much effort,
to maintain an equilibrium behaviour...
not high, not too low,
so that, next time if I am down too...
the front, anonymous or known, can't say —
"You are changed," seems like an allegation.

Another thing is that —
I may be much more,
but I will be showing myself as a noob, slobby, and uninteresting,
so that they may not get attracted too much to me,
and which will automatically not lead to predominantly consuming my precious time,
forget about others!!
even my personal time with me.

The above two are for the people,
but for you, Girl, you are a teacher...
of automatically behaving well.
I will try to show you even exceeding...
whatever I am not,
whatever I am not practicing,
you are an eliminator of suspicion, a certain drive in my life,
 (lucky mascot),

that's why I am like before after.
I cannot neglect you,
Girl!!
Instances will fulfil a book,
I am not a dreamer; I am a doer.
"Tunes of Time... Incessant you," in practical...
would be written on you.
It's my perception and in my life never-ending your chapter.
Who the hell other than me is so divine on this earth?
another greatest lover???
from scrap to whatever I have achieved of you,
I think after my life too would be thus a never-ending matter...
In the pages too, my words will love the entire covered emotions of you...
Every emotion in depth is our chatter, which will be filled with how a lover behaved in love,
to other lovers.

It Seems Like

I was hesitant to face the opposite sex.

I understood the girl's maximum for further future...
by the name of you, with time elapsed with you,
(thanks for the experience).
That's not the case.
Nothing is indeed in front of you,
in lieu of you,
maximum tries done on you,
maximum I am engaged.
Now,
I am something and much more with you,
that's why you reciprocate,
otherwise publicly meeting you,
so casually, was not so without hindrance.
Or messages with you,
to improve my communication skills anytime,
without having you beside,
were going to be limited or jot
(only work-related).

I am too top-notch in males,
otherwise!!
the concerns of others were given a thought,
and it's ok,
that's why I immensely worked on myself,
befitting better in every aspect a male should be...
thus, expecting you,
the suitor numbers were to be,

by me... curtailed.

Choose me,
I am not a rascal and opportunist,
I will love you,
like when I will be unable to love you,
like with my all capabilities.

There is a total before and after by in-between you.
You defined me,
that's why much and more,
we will live happily hereafter.
See, gratitude to you now has to become the case,
like a parent, my mirth becomes imprisoned in jail!
when I see not to bother me,
something pesky you are hiding from me.
You become sick; I become pale,
never felt you so special when you needed,
without expecting any gains...
that's the true love of me,
I can't see the sad part of you,
which for you entails.

Your scooty stops there somewhere,
on the same day,
my bike battery goes in vain.
How come Girl!!
 Just as non-biological things are like acting insane??

500 rupees you gave to a needy/greedy or heart-wrenching actor's
acting don't know... whom!!
but disclosed to me,
the very next morning, the police on Carter Road,

cut a 500 rupees challan,
like for without a helmet, visiting sea face.
What the heck!!
Frequently in the past ten months, I went there and then!
never ever, but how come on gloomy mornings at 6:00 am,
they, that day, came?

There is a connection, small and big,
perceived interconnected to water...
just as sardines and whales.
There are many!!
Why to describe so personally personal?
 but just as they are going, it seems like...
next time you will get your periods,
Girl, I will be too getting,
and would be the first male,
and you will help me out at every aspect of my first time very gently.

I love you... I love you... I love you insanely, madly, and badly...
in any correlation or relation haphazardly.
No chance my thoughts for you with any weather would ever change.

Scent Of Sweat

Any Tom, Dick, and Harry...
praises and lauds me,
it is a — thank you!
Nothing none-other any exponential growth of...
happy hormones in me.

I hope by this same instance!
knowing an ordinary man like me,
she must be feeling like...
Tom, Dick, and Harry, (at present),
applauding her,
in hiding of me.

But I pray to God,
I believe in my scent of sweat,
that becoming something,
even to this whole aura around or to the world,
then too... the most precious is still and will be...
career oriented, that bold girl!
marked with her bold decision.
(Same person as me), if I laud her,
even or on a bit of her achievement...
she must serve herself a genuine glee.

I know in the subconscious,
meanwhile, in-between...
all the things are done by me,
is indirectly due to her.
To present myself in front of her with confidence,

if I came in front intimidating to others with my identity,
in me, her probability and proximity derived all the achievement,
my life's agenda must be.

Love will impart as a hot surface and cold surface interact, and will attain mutual equilibrium.
Everything would be mutual when the subconscious signalled and hard work would be...
on becoming me as the best version possible of mine,
that's nothing like begging for a request,
it's obviously me.
So, best selective and without hassle, process for her too...
so, may I be the suitor in true love engaging her,
no clues, no chance,
no one would take over me.

I Will Presume Your Mental Health, Just Your Motor Units Misfired

Whatever you will do,
unconditionally, I will love you,
always told you.

I will assume your mental health,
motor units misfired!
they opted reverse, averse between like synonyms,
or alike, maybe they opted antonyms.
"Yes" to complete "no", didn't get...
to elaborate on yourself maybe!
Dark room was not the thing maybe, but...
just switched by a newbie like,
frisking the walls,
as binary (0 or 1) like nothing to do between...
mind just with intention 1, just clicked wrong.

Many a time, this disheartening condition happens,
(like in my childhood it happened).
When someone admiring,
is taking care of each one, pleasantries, discussing anecdotes, laughing
at cousin's marriage sudden meet,
you are waiting for your turn sitting.
When he/she comes to you,
even saying "let's go to market" neglecting all,
I would say no,
in confusion, but internally it was yes.
Or,
I am craving for him/her!

how come he/she read it?
Is there on my face a colour or hue...
that I caught begging for attention.
It happens in humans, admit it,
I will assume it for you too.

To me, it was like —
An elder brother or especially my favourite cousin sister,
now not been to India for many years,
that's why I think for the future too...
then I craved her togetherness and attention,
that much, then too, in advance.
Same after meeting with each one at a function came to me.
Hey!!
"Let's go to the market to buy some bricks of ice cream."
I myself was going to spend time with her,
don't know what crossed my mind, insane,
and I abruptly said no!!
(which was two hours later).
I said no!
"I have some work of cylinder pick up from the market,
you go for your concern, *Didi*,"
her eyes were a bit sparkling...
I overcame but was unable to tell my cousin sorry,
for that petty thing, which at that time was a thing.

 Any erratic behaviour yes to complete no!
I will forgive you for that incident only.
 Your hesitant behaviour is big yes, actually...
what people will think is the work of you.
With glum face or glee, you will put me in dejection or sorrow whatever, but...
in reference to my childhood with my Didi,

and that child of mine in you, I love you...
 even to what extent you will be pesky.
 In many things, I have learned much more,
 even eye contact and continuing with confidence, relevant talks, and social skills,
 are all due to talks, texts, and interaction with,
 a strong girl who I know by the name of you.

It's ok,
it happens many times, person becomes erratic,
and it's simple it's just a 100 out of 1 layer or nuance of you,
you are a beautiful person, average or...
maximum should be good,
it's not like every time you will make it...
but I promise, as you and me are now mutual,
if no audacity,
I will somehow gently,
refine you too...
like you did immensely in percentage much more to me.

Actually, Factually And Really

Everything is stagnant in their place,
but it has a switch.
Out of 80,
20 received, completing 100 perceived.
You are just memorizing bad memories...
despite maximum good (which is 80).
This will decide the tenure of the person,
is he/she going to reside longer,
or that's it!
that's enough for you.

Even the subconscious needs feeding,
choose wisely all the instances, glimpses, instincts, and footprints
where to go,
thus, eliminate or include internally too...
if not majorly,
but really, it's up to you.

(Writer unknown) but,
In *Kuch Kuch Hota Hai,* king of romance, SRK says —
"Hum jeete ek baar hai,
  Marte Ek baar hai,
  Pyar bhi Ek hi baar hota hai."
According to his that time theory,
and point of view, it's true!
"Indulge in one" whatever.

Averse, reverse,
In Dear Zindagi (writer unknown) but SRK says —

"Don't have a creaky kursi" (chair),
like make experience of sittings,
thus, comfort and compatibility checking...
means take time, have options, seeing compatibility,
don't indulge in one, or thus choose the wrong one...
for a whole life or life long, don't be hasty.
(Writer unknown) but one person SRK's,
dual thoughts!!
Now in this too...
what to choose,
what to rationalize,
or take away message,
indulge in one or distribute your phone's battery/energy,
it's too up to you...
but,
what SRK taught if it's important to you,
(writer unknown) but a person...
at two points he is — with two points of view.

How Much???

How much talent, time, ecstasy,
conscious alertness needed to...
impress you!!

Rather I would be silent.
I need my time lonely to muse.
It's better,
rather than allied with interest,
repeated you...

Actually, I get discharged,
while seeing a negative force like you.

It Is Happening

It's happening to you, congrats!
(Binge in the time),
receive the accolades...
if it was not happening to you,
they were unable to recognize,
it too :)

Strenuous Strides / Partial Killings

Strenuous strides, alert human mind, gasping, internally derived, short of breath, pesky draining,
are all partial killings that I am giving to myself...
to live longer,
and to cut the path long left,
of my dreams.

Especially so that, the slogan and poems written by me and myself,
from atom to the entirety,
can get some actual meanings.

English Too Is A Superfine, Beautiful And Blissful Language

English too is a superfine, beautiful language,
as a writer, I came to know,
with its beautiful instincts.

Before writing, compiling, and publishing my book,
"TUNES OF TIME... Incessant You,"
reading...
The Penguin Book of Indian poets,
a compilation of...
(famous and acknowledged 90 poets),
best in their lifetime given,
selected from each poet, five poems best,
many of them are no more with their rhymes and words left.

But I don't think, I would be able to complete it,
in a limited time,
whenever I think about reading 25 pages as a discipline daily at least,
my mind lures me to go into my character and write my own English...
but it's good when I would be going to distract myself from overthinking,
I will go through this masterpiece...
thus, my mental engine by other's divine words will calm down,
but I think!
Who knows his language,
(the mother tongue),
but not the one written in the book respected,
with best feelings by chance,
what humongous he is missing!!

Just as my father says,
many times, to learn Bengali,
so that I may relish the creation of Rabindranath Tagore,
in its original form like Geetanjali.
Words have power,
say it against a tyrant,
like 'Vande Mataram' of Bankim.
I always wonder!
in Hindi, English don't know yet,
but in current use,
in the population of 800 crore of the world, there are 7115 languages
in this present time!
There are approximately 1,70,000 words in the English Oxford
Dictionary!
How the words aggregate, accumulate, and design themselves including
phonetics...
and adjusts for a meaning?
From a plot, then a conclusion, and describing everything,
how everyone unanimously accepted,
the confabbed voice, tune, or sound and what it would connote as its
meaning.
Who bound all diction first in the dictionary?
first time to know up to now, how it is recorded so fine.

Who made these words from the Palaeolithic Ages to present?
How 26 alphabets from A to Z, engendered one lakh seventy thousand
words with their proper unanimous meanings?
and so proper, more enhanced dictum and sayings.

Further, how verses and poems are derived!
 It's not only about ending the poetry on lines,
on the "e" or "d" alphabet to make a rhyme,

but how do English/Hindi/Marathi/Bengali/Telugu/Hebrew,
like every language adjusts the meaning to suffice!

Best poetry always every time engages me to think more,
that I am being helped by...
someone more than me and subconscious me, and my conscience,
especially all the relevant, being a poet,
 escaping irrelevant, how it comes to mind?
Literally, I took my hand in sudden shock on my head and pressed it
tight two-three and a lot more times.
That how this word, this idea came so proper,
in a proper place at so proper time.
Practicing for since long,
having experience with 2500+ poetry written,
by my own hands is another thing,
but I can't gauge many a time.

But approximately every language has got this prosperous, prosperity to
have a meaningful tome,
like how???
how???
So... engaging, ethereal, eternal...
How perfect is humankind??

If the next 50 years upcoming...
I will be writing 50 books.
Then too, it will amaze me amazingly,
being a lover of words — Logophile.

Penuiry Is Exactly Reverse To Divine

From 11:30 PM to 12:30 AM, late-night running!
Not a record, but 8 km daily approximate run, since...
the last ten days taught me. 👇

With a lesson like,
you should not each and every time...
be thankful for a matter.
Brand new shoes, sole abraded...
due to regular running friction,
and this roughly tortured non-living in a sulk...
given a good fine.
When the bike is off due to...
(4°cold and bike battery matter),
shoes being worn out soles and no grip much,
resulting in no more friction,
slithered badly and hurt my ankle, badly with the kick... iron matter.

Change the shoes!
have a new battery!
or schedule yourself for attention for a proper angle to kick when hasty!
Assiduity and hard work of running 8 km daily in one hour for ten days approximately...
now have given options!

Plus, one more –
Life is a clutter,
of the pros and cons :),
a fitness level attained with less mirth but actually pain,

with to be ankle hair fracture, when a kick was generated,
now demands...
the best quality "Calcium Citrate Malate" supplement,
too... for joints better protein consumption,
otherwise, now joints are going to suffer for the personal betterment
interchanged by lethal excruciations.

A triple way of 'no way out' expense:
A new shoe,
my feet want a new renewal.
Bike needs battery change for climate acclimatization.
And body demands for recovery supplementation.
Now hard work and versus hard work, comes a calculation!!
If I have money!!
Otherwise, leisure and rest are the chills, and all I need...
there is no barter system,
(like... you will give 4 kg rice to get 1 kg of cylinder gas, is not the system.)
Only money is the map for whatever you think...
and definitely for further.
Above there is the triple sensation of wrap with hindrance,
 otherwise, there is the simplest one blanket wrap on the cot of laziness.
So, the gist is —
Hard work too needs a monetary drive,
 there is no barter system like said...
(like... you will give 4 kg rice to get 1 kg of cylinder gas).
So, rather than to be degraded in destitution, and taunts of extra mental degradations,
it's better if you are pompous...
and with others snobby,
or whatever as a result of scornful abbreviations.

3 – 4 Hour Personal Time

To be successful,
I have already changed my 24-hour circadian cycle,
in reference to 90 percent of the Indian population.
Rather than night for some personal dreams,
I sleep in the afternoon time,
but then too…
at the end of the 24-hour circadian cycle,
I muse about –
I could have done much more.

After some time, I will be damn successful.
Yes, sure as my intuitions are,
hard work is the scent of sweat,
imminently imminent just soon…
in the coming time.

Then life will be too not easy,
or will be going to get easy…
or will be easy.
Then the problem would be –
Why the heck!!
those people waiting to be but at present…
surely unsuccessful as the former me,
are so impedance in my fruitful,
which I so waited to enjoy,
flourishing dream time???
It will shock me…
more because I was an admirer,
I was not of that kind.

Expectations will increase for help,
new relations released will fall in the lap,
for reference for further, but if not done like...
with sarcastic remarks and much more than snides!
The home address is already known on Google too,
Then in a thousand... one case they will pelt something like!
or will be there for the demand like —
Yes, like my father with me went to some personalities for a bright future of mine, many years back like.

By the way both physically and mentally,
in the gym and library, both included...
I work 18+ hours a day,
and I am vigilant about...
not more than five hours of my sleeping time.

But see if by taking another person's case too —
(Nine hours) say is the duty time,
(one hour) went in up-down total from home to office like,
(two hours) all total including ablution, dressing up, eating, and all,
(one hour) for health and fitness,
(eight hours) sleep taken.
~~~~~~~~~~
It comes to 21 hours already in calculations.
The rest I will read or write,
or will give time to making a different income stream,
or will simply be three hours, it's for my mom/dad and most beloved wife.

To some genuine definitely, I can't deny,
but for rest —
who the heck are you (I can't say),
but that's life.

And after writing this piece,
the power of this piece is —
I am too now simply uninterested in demanding help,
and already retreated for the hope of supply.
Yes, if needed support or help, then too I will do it,
on my own,
if they can solve then too...
no demands from some superiors,
being a subordinate to them in the meantime,
or even to my subordinates in the meanwhile.

Let everyone pursue or think free,
or be with only some special ones in that three-four hours left personal time.

No Rule Withstands

Life is so unpredictable,
that no rule withstands...
proper to the other while testing,
that's the — beauty and dementia of life,
the ingenuity in understanding it is...

The ingenuity in understanding it is...
every whole proper and single saying or dictum is,
with amalgamation of averse, reverse,
more proper seeming lines.

The Power Of This Piece

The mediocrity of a substance is decided by its time elapsed in comfort...
and I have not.
It's my intelligence, and non-sloppy behaviour of mine,
to become time-taking damn impeccable!
that's why they are not barking at me,
before this, some quaked my mental toughness,
now by my progress...
I being an agenda,
quake their mental peace.

When I was average,
do this, do that, then comes – not fit.
So, I decided,
going to do something different...
demands will rise from elsewhere,
and everywhere,
in a bigger proportion.
I need no mercy,
dice will turn according to my will...
no connotation of weak,
(is myself),
is the power of this piece.

To pacify the chaos of "what if,"
always thinking the opposite of the done...
and experience in your mind, the misfortune, and taunts accolated,
which it could have brought,
that is the mental trick.

I Am Ready To Kill Or Die

I am ready to kill or die,
anyway...in front of me is too a beast in hide,
but better it's not the matter of venom test,
or brawn strength or mettle,
whatever the allegations are...
if definitely, both of us will die.
One thing is pretty clear,
not that my kind of intelligence for the future of this country, at least.

Should neglect and not to jeopardize his life,
on this trivial, egoistic, deadly fight.
Not in wine, no utopia, no imagination,
but rather no fear in foreseen summarised.

I will escape, maybe,
like a coward, no problem.
How I ran...
then faltered, fell, or stumbled,
whatever!
let it be the timeline.
To write one year per book,
until defeated and succumbed to death,
so that,
the last, most experienced, would be divine.

Rather than an uncouth and illiterate culture developing misogynist...
jibber-jabber of...MC, BC, JC, DC receptor and,
with amplification public blabber in a day... 17 times.

So, the gist is,
I am more hyper, sane, seer, and desperate underlined.

English Shairy 102ish

Dreadful things are not dreading anymore,
the entirety is different,
fellows are different.

Actually, factually, and eventually...
"Like you there are many",
it's true!
but I don't hear it nowadays,
often.

Because I have done,
something in the meantime,
and sorry, thus...
did not give them the accessibility.

Yes, I Am A Poet

Yes, I am a Poet,
insomniac, unable to sleep,
I am slow in action,
not due to lethargy.

But I think "Poets" and "Shayars,"
or every intellectual in the thought process profound, humongous are this way like...
and should be or like this,
working, crumbling, destructing, distributing, and forming,
many ascensions and downfalls...
and gauging all calculations all the time,
then forming into a specific creation described in a structural form underlined.

My mind is working superfast,
so, in the action there is shunting...
well, it's all scientific, meanwhile.

Just as when you eat,
(contemporary or maybe a bit later),
all blood flows maximum to the digestive system,
with hormonal changes too...
you feel sleep-like...
when you workout,
it rushes fast toward your skeletal, voluntary muscles,
that's why your face and other too...
becomes red at workout.
Only one thing at a time...
 in body there too, it is an internal policy, settings,

and it's called shunting.
Majorly one goal, one agenda as a given deadline.

Three day's workout at one time,
not push, pull, legs...
but legs + legs + legs,
will make you, no matter how much beast you are,
if done properly, not available but assailable,
even your base of support would be faltering,
like a ramshackle building,
at that given point...
in future with no hopes to thrive.
Same way —
We or I, being a Poet, thinking or excruciating our limited brain to a next level,
makes us tired,
loss of cognition and assailable...
and it's all internal, not making a face,
especially day time is the recovering hours or maybe pensive pen's working hours,
so, don't mess with us at our weak time,
we are already with cumulative sleepless nights,
especially if lost... no taunts, no snide remarks, or ribbing...
from here to there with a thought if we are rambling,
not being under-confident, not neglecting but,
sunken shoulders, kyphotic posture, pensive head, gaze down entails pensive pen,
that's it.
I or we, are not maximum vigil outside,
many a times internally vigil,
don't withdraw our attention,
otherwise...
we are impregnable and it's a warning!
we are furious with lost lines.

Who Said Self-Doubt, Insecurities Are Not Good

Many self-doubts were there,
Impregnable thoughts were cluttered!
It is an atomic habit to jot down on a paper,
I knew it was me versus this world,
for being occupied, alienated, and being ill later,
to cooldown frustration and temper, it's better.

But not even doing a Ph.D. or not even the smallest course...
why I came into English literature?
writing three to four-page poems.
Going like averse, from my like mother tongue, Hindi,
after writing 100s, 1000 couplets in it meanwhile later!!
Being in muse mode,
I thought enough, enough...
conclusion came —
Whatever I write is maximum time personally personal,
it's like my personal diary, not imagination.
Yes, what people think or will think, being an author too...
I can't subside!
So, being and continuing then the agenda and addiction to write,
my agenda was not to describe the confidential things.
No way!!
So, that someone at random may singe my soft side.
It's so far not just an artistic matter,
inclination towards,
revealing my crush, relationship, plans, and exposure.
That's why derivation may turn into mockery or mock,
clean chit from her,

ethical, open-minded, she is...
but the legit truth is,
I cannot trespass, person's personal,
or it's a mutual understanding that at least not that much.
I was to obfuscate in a good and decent meaning,
some sort of people and friends,
who personally were opportunity seekers,
never was it that much, I am trying to be...
high class or top-notch by my vocabulary and meanings,
or English is more global, more exposure was there,
was not that much in my subconscious mind,
but instead of "Shers" with the same intensity,
knack English "Couplets" would be more confidential,
from a selected crowd,
who never mugged 4000 words and numerous books,
while being me honing my mind in another language,
that was English and inculcating new skills,
because they were not friends,
maximum of them were... the treacherous, clowns, and backbiters.
She was and is a cynosure, beautiful with a superlative degree man,
but what about ten versus I?
If written daily, the content on love connotation may derive in easy
language an easy meaning, an inclination...
I loved her and needed her all the time,
no misogyny at the same time.
Reading not like a newspaper on Instagram/Facebook, but privacy so
that through writings being a published author previously,
others may not connote the wrong dictums, over a girl...
especially so to curtail the musing crowd on Instagram/Facebook,
in my arsenal, there were too many bombs and crackers,
but why to waste time and energy on manageable or trivial matters?

Yes, I accept and acknowledge that,
many things generalized in my mind, maximum...
maybe it was not up to that extent,
outside it was minimum,
then too...
I was in fear of shame, fear of ignominy, being a subject of good or bad ribbing, taunts, being understood as weak, peer pressure.
Yes actually, factually, and eventually,
 all of these are not zigzag, but all these were...
merely my insecurities.
Which led me to learn English and without doing anything,
I am not good, but great at English poems and newsletters too... I found later.
So, all compound remarkably making, in the next two months, me an English Author of my book —
"Tunes of Times... Incessant You",
 now in the next two months with my own published in English after Hindi,
 getting remarks from maximum...
who doesn't know how to write even a page,
in their life, even in their mother tongue,
will criticize my book,
would be hilarious!!

But wait a minute!!
So, it's good, no??
Shame, fear of ignominy, being a subject of good or bad ribbing,
taunts, being understood as weak, peer pressure.

All good, no???

Who said self-doubt, and insecurities are not good???

Who said — "what would people say?"
"Fear", not good???

Answer me.

I Am Tank Infront of Guns

Failure fillips me,
gives me reverse effects that now,
I am not afraid of,
any boy or men,
(except for the unconscious drunkard).

In the same field, who will be for being or standing at No.1,
being my best competitor,
can thrash me, break my leg...
I am already in Mumbai,
courage and boldness with all from Gurgaon,
to prove to my father,
it matters the most,
audacities of life...
lonely shrieks and peaks of like an apocalypse due to me, myself, and
my demanding life in silence, made me audacious,
and in me, it's the constant clime.
I forgot all the shame,
afraid of popularity!
Let me be a cynosure,
one bread is the need for life on starvation, and whether...
outside there are tanks and guns like.

I can eat well and can get married,
I can go well off...
with whatever talent I have,
my whole life...
but that's not the gist of my foreseen life.
I will grind...

to prove to my mother,
it matters the most.
Many times, negative thoughts, and whims comes randomly, extremely.
Yes, I will be achieving for sure all,
but making my place will seem like...
I am replacing all and old benchmarks toppling.
If killed by one versus me, or ten versus me,
with the seemed effects of dominating, intimidating, taking away the opportunities of someone,
which was not by an invading outsider, me.
Then the other thought, whim comes,
then too... ok.
I may be inspiring or demoralizing,
whatever conclusion, choose it.
My work is my work, that's it.
It's now quivering turned fearless me...
whatever may come,
I may be the culprit,
but,
for my better future,
and the content of my parents, my ambitions,
and the test of coming, to Mumbai, what derived me.
If danger is fruitful, give me.
Never went 4-5 kilometres above with bike,
to investigate and enjoy the city.
I am alone, with no time in making friends,
just reading and writing.

If an outsider or known person comes,
he/she posts sea view, spots, etc.
Rambling like came to Macca daily, it's ok.
Invites me to meet, but I am really busy...
I am poor me.

Every time thoughtful and overthinker in me,
carries a piece of baggage (in my ambits or locked in a room),
that,
how much more I can jot down my own written story.
Even after being cloyed then too...
revising, rewriting, and overwriting in the same room incessantly.

Yes, I will achieve something,
or will try incessantly...
and will go from here loving myself for trying hard,
from here to heaven with no back down wholeheartedly.

2500+ dialogues and poems already written,
will continue to 3000,
then 4000... let's see,
which count in this world, defines me.

Yes, it's me.

Yes, You Are A Personality Development Course

Yes, you are a personality development course.
The practice that I am getting with the encounter and talking regularly with you,
definitely, it's going to revise and better me,
my confidence has elapsed with a girl top-notch, says all that...
I am too of a standard,
but believe me!
it is not a practice to be comfortable or good at communication and then,
the intention of applying that...
to another person of the previously shy me,
who turned an extrovert due to you.
I am not a good actor of any kind,
rather than opposing the former me in front of you...
meek, naive, and under-confident former me,
says thank you always for whatever your grace has made me.
The party averse is now a party animal,
by interacting and practicing, so with practice and regular invasions with the clans there with glee...
then too –
Rather than this,
the perspective/picture is totally different,
the whole scene is reversed.
Decoration of words claims,
no short replies but elaborated emails...
frequency of talks with topics in my mind,
out of the blue came,
sometimes still...

cracking, fumbling, and breaking voice like you are a star or celebrity
and obviously very respected.
How I talk to you with respect, surrender, and support, and your
future gains,
all even while going in recent rewinds enthral me.

All symbolize; I think it clarifies a girl too...
a boy's stance or simply my true addiction for you.
After all, you are a beautiful human,
not a beautiful mural painting.
With human emotions from long ago you have on this Earth
experienced,
including the sudden and exponentially change in me.
I am erratic and maybe unexpectedly inexperienced,
but my likeness, my fondness for you goes deep down...
please, if possible, to connect with you,
I mean in the imminent time, I mean in two-three days,
please gauge... how much from just being friends,
that —
I am inclined towards loving you...
by reciprocating,
not obviously in the context of...
"Friends with benefits,"
but, in the way of platonic love, please...
reward me,
then make it your instincts.

No Feel Of Pro,
Just Giving My Best,
No Novice

Every painful bleeding only gives you laud, applause of valour like...
the person confabbing laud may matter.

When not!!
Enjoy and depress yourself simultaneously many times,
but —
When many and many times it would be a "sign wave" of...
you being lucky or hapless (unlucky),
you will listen (from surroundings),
according to the fluctuations in your life.
You will develop proper endurance and strength,
to let things go meanwhile...
seen, observed, degraded, upgraded...
what you are... what you are not!
No feel of a pro,
Just giving best, no novice.
Any imminently coming or passing thing...
will not give you compassion or if will hurt with its biased nature,
then too... you would be ok.
Towards you now, it will throw of its... lesser and lesser percentage,
it would be an equilibrium state.
With lesser and lesser fluctuations,
with time elapsed identified.
"I think you have not felt the poetry,
but my gist is defined."
I mean like a stone thrown in the middle of a river,

versus a stone N times much bigger, in the middle of an ocean.
Ocean never shows a character of undergoing on the banks; that's so fine.

If not still,
you will feel...
when you will inculcate elderhood from adulthood with time.
A single cell then into a zygote derived from copulation...
became so big by multiplication,
there was not a single neuron, verdict, or conscience,
but now!
your eyeballs are bigger than that primitive one... a trillion/infinite time.
Unknown nature too gave you time,
so, flow with the rhyme.

Or I will perspire more by the mind,
and would add some lines for better to comprehend or stability of the rhymes later in this piece,
to better clarify.

Full Means Full, Complete Every Time, Even No Odd Or Ish

I am not in front of or affront, not even contemplated right now,
just having my self-time in carving.
Some big and numerous medium and denser, many small or low...
I cannot deal so...
in my words, it's cunning,
will come all of a sudden,
to have a fight with obviously being big,
only with the big few.
The other small bed bugs should not and will not tarnish my body
after a heavy battle while sleeping.
Just the right time, I am being proficient; I am profoundly focused,
with a full plan, I am searching.
I need a sound sleep which will result in cognition,
better to take decisions against present much bigger,
and...
whether it's forging a sword in the future,
or say —
180 words in 180 minutes, if I can learn and imbibe,
and if that's it!
I need the most relevant,
whether it's time, need of aura, concentration, convenience, or
whatever...
nothing should bother other than that,
nothing should diminish,
no other topics.
My work plan is...
I mean it's critical and crucial to choose the energy to be invested in
selected enemies too...
full means full, complete every time, even...
no odd or "Ish".

That's Why, I Am Showing

The poetry you want to read, relish, and imbibe many a time,
layer by layer your mind further will not support the same texture!
and it's ok.
That's it...
how fickle, natural with caprice is a human mind!!
For a person, this may be the same,
enjoyment of the other may depend on the situation derived,
situation settings may change...
and he may not be the same continuing in the continuum, meanwhile.
That's why I am showing still. my dearest...
that, why you are still to me my lifeline!!

That your infatuation for the perceived present person real,
 may break anytime.
And in lieu of that,
I am the best...
you can decide.

Dante Alighieri

Whatever I got of you was a dream,
from where I was a random stalker of you,
I will acknowledge it a million times,
that's how, and that's it.
What if??
if I was unable to get the time, the duration...
with whatever you were mine,
that's how I kill the repugnance and penitence of if deeds done or the way of,
why you are not continuing the same divine.

In one word, publicly I am a follower turned to whom you follow (on Instagram), in a short while,
in the 100s who tried!
that's the adage, in front and truth...
of my achievement,
in this cult time.

100 hours approximately, 100 sessions in four-five months I gave you, personal training so fine...
every proximity of ours is still reminiscent and in my mind reclined.
I know,
you are not an avid reader,
but go deeper on – "DANTE ALIGHIERI", an Italian poet of the 12th century who met his love only two times,
at the age of 18-19, and before that at 8-9,
and he is the greatest one of each benchmark in poetics, with the imagination and reality of his...
one-sided love "BEATRICE,"

with only those two instances!
Then why not me?
I am beyond dimensions and dimensionless then...
see how much I got you with you and me making memories,
at our pleasure full time,
versus him!!
with one time playing with her @ 8-9,
when Dante was nine and Beatrice was eight, in a garden (where he fell in love).
In between just and just searching but never got a peek or glance of her until the last, at the age of 18 and his 19,
on the banks of river; just a passing smile.
And see, we are still continuing with probability in our 30's,
where she at the age of 22, giving pains and pangs to him with only those two meetings,
sorry to say she discontinued life.
Then too... she was the inspiration and only inspiration for up to his last book, "The Divine Comedy,"
40 years after her lifetime.
True Love in magnitude and intensity is just defined.
So...
So, what if I didn't sleep with you?
Thus, in minimal and minimum, the done magnitude maximum of my thoughts with you, obsessively insane,
is totally legit defined.

I know I am a person of my own aura, importance, and air,
but don't know!!
why do I feel so special by your words, mutual interests, must-needed talks, pleasantries, and all each one...
one by one combined!
and thus, my fate is not in hope but a surefire guarantee of one day getting you...

I go to know you in those 100 hours an innumerable time,
such as all blueprints are ready with absolutely no misguide.
I am a very optimistic person and positive person; here I show it.
Any negative thing on my mission I will omit,
will not consider myself belonging to it, even in front of my eye.
To define it in my way — that's how the "Law of Attraction" works...
 and that's how,
one day your arms are wide open saying to me to clasp you,
and you will be mine... in the imminent time.

Likewise

Whatever colour, form, or salon...
she has curly or straight, blonde, short,
she has her hair.
Likewise,
a tear sparkling in my eyes,
with low to high magnitude...
it always confirms me,
there is she —
not a newcomer, no novice.

I am a heroic thing, true, like crying...
and she is strong enough not to emote herself,
regardless of my reflected implores and emotions,
then too not seldom, often, but always beautiful.

If I don't get her, then too... from one side,
if I get her, then, divine.
She is the dearest thing...
will be eternally, ethereally,
dearest to me for a lifetime.

Include, Preclude, Conclude Or Exclude I Am Yours From My Way Intrigued

How come the dearest thing you are to me,
you don't know!
No human or animal has the same feel.
Your elemental thing is that,
your nicety over me is over-cute,
include, preclude, conclude, or exclude...
I am yours from all my way intrigued.
Enormously many sulks, anxiety, and length of long, each hour of
working at the office,
extremely extinguishes and completely diminishes at the end of every
dart thrown; face on my mental sanity shuts up.
24 hours is quite less time, each second with you is my wish each time.
Yes, I work only so that we may not go destitute,
when it comes to confab with you,
when it comes to your face —
your day... how was it???
you blab all, that's my reward!!!
I have to solve and that's the best selfless me,
with you in solitude.

Many sulks comprehended similar to cantankerous shrieks are
oblivious and forgiven, because of you,
because this happens when,
frustration is likely lesser than excitement, when you are by my side.
Continuing whatever, but at the end of somewhere, there comes a
commencement of you,

otherwise, meanwhile, in the meantime, it was an ill thing over and over,
next day ready to bite,
with an incurred magnitude derived.

Your face, your talks, your dilemma, your confusion, apprehensions on what went wrong, your recovery, your all —
not soothe...
extremely soothe it is.
One-third work, one-third sleep (condition applied), one-third directly, indirectly maximum you,
and there it lies.
That's it!!
I am in 24-hour's best use,
and it's divine.

You are a remedy,
flabbergasting and celebrated each time.
You are raw and new,
each time with an undented hue.
Just being a friend —
no issues (let it be inter-caste),
you from your side arranged,
from my side, love.
Your family is decent,
my family is decent,
they like you,
Girl, I will marry you.
Immensely without self-respect even after marriage,
I would say each moment, "I love you,"
a million times.
Saying yes!!
was a very cute consent,

thankful behaviour of you.
Ultimately, I am a one-woman man,
with all condiments, ingredients, and package, one and only...
whole life I will prove that I am yours,
 you are mine.
A little later you will also fall in love with me,
a little more or as much as I do,
seeing your inclination, I absolutely know.

 So, absolutely no issues,
 take your time...
then too you will be a moon,
 and I will be a fan of you...
and it would be,
endline of my lifetime.

Your Number Of Brothers Doesn't Matter To Me

I am very fortunate to still be talking to you,
Girl, you don't know!!
you are the sweetest craving, like...
 being at the peak or the acme of "diabetes mellitus,"
if I will taste you as I will die certainly,
then too...

If suppose high BP, Hypertension (scientific name),
I want to see you,
with a sudden glance, bringing up a high surge in me,
and whether it's... that's it.
Then too... thank you.

Girl, you just say "Yes,"
your number of brothers doesn't matter to me...
I can die by their hands,
if instead of my true love,
they can't have any mercy.

If you marry someone else,
not mere... but maximum chances!
in the instalment of pain and tears,
then too you don't know...
I am no more —
without any cunning.

That's why, before being hapless (unlucky),
I should, and I want to do a favour with my life.
In both cases, it seems the case and scenarios are the same...
so, where there are and will be no probable forwards with you,
I just want no caprice too in the future to rewind.
New memories in making there should be,
each day with you.

Shed a tear, that's it...
 my conclusion is distinctly clear:
"Come what may,"
I can't play on probability.
You are mine...
not a jot of haplessness nocturnal or diurnal without you...
like the Sun for life, you are my sunshine.

Never Blame Yourself With A Lucky Tag

Never blame yourself with a lucky tag.
I comprehend and understand a lot,
everything may have repercussions later.
Being an author, writer, blogger — whatever,
neglecting the assiduity aside,
many a time not, but mostly I quiver,
literally... quiver!
and my pen opts to dismiss many mature, relevant thoughts.
Suppose the words written in thousand versus,
the only one or two which may be other than or over than
inappropriate and taunting...
for a soft-hearted other,
which was just making a plot for the scenario and was not any other matter.
Then see apprehensively or hypothetically what happened actually,
what I got —
If sleeping 2 or 3, or 4 hours for straight three days,
due to the bombardment of thoughts that I had to jot down a lot,
fourth day is the confrontation at the night,
according to and affording their suitable time,
and the whole day is busy,
cramped with appointments and meetings,
I am sleep-deprived,
and human tendency belongs to it.
I am injurious to the mental state of others,
whether I am of that kind or not,
I may blab without having even a wine.
With what I have written or with reference,

my mental sanity is the cost,
which with the sufferance of other's questioning and nit-picking and
detrimental minds, is going to be worst,
in which they are not.
A lonely bird flying high got the sharpest arrows because I was glanced
a lot.
This time, I only need survival,
don't overload me...
and too... I am not the person dented by you,
I will not plead... but how come it's not??
The dogs may bark intentionally that...
if the lion is or will not be sleeping fourth night,
rather than only sleep-deprived.
They are mature without doing much,
with all his belongings and him,
at the asylum he will have the lunch,
and that's the win-win chime.

Thus, A Street Dog Seems Like An Injurious Lion Indeed Without Doing Anything.

The secret behind being an English Poet, Writer,
and one day or the other publishing my English book "Tunes of Time"
are these 4007... vocabulary/words, (which I can't show you in this paper view).
But this is my fourth notebook which you cannot see,
like this, each ended up around 1000-1000 words.
For others it may simply seem as clutter but,
whenever I read books, related to English literature (a long list),
with my curious mind, I found and wondered what that means??
I underlined it, checked it on the Sahni Dictionary,
then cross-checked it on Google and noted it down...
with how to use it in a sentence.
Maximum work on this was done in and around 2015,
when I was (bed-ridden) unable to walk well and properly due to left knee ACL (Anterior Cruciate Ligament) surgery.
When I got injured by only 90 kg, in the exercise Clean and Jerk —
that weight which I was able to do 90 times in a session, at JLN Stadium, Delhi at sport weightlifting.

That's why probably, I am afraid of even the simplest things now,
and the hyena seems like an injurious lion indeed,
that dead and non-living matter with no grudges and emotions did this...
my weightlifting career and workout were totally hampered for a total of 1.5 years.
The time didn't elapse, by this period I used it...

going to revise all, plus add on...
how much mental sweat is and was perspired, I don't know, but I wiped it...
who knows the future laureate in the making.

That's It Now, Abstract Things All Fallen In Pace

Ooo... wooo... wooo...!!
What is this out-of-the-world abbreviation, havoc English, vocabulary,
and all you are with?

Then the question asked is – to impress??
(Now it seems better).
To upgrade their knowledge; having a curious mind,
if capable of matching my mind,
which is probably excruciating,
and thus, I am eating their promotion letters.
Ya, better than...
in a monologue or on stage,
hindering me in between,
and saying, "Get your facts right,"
and each time that humiliation in front of others,
afore torture culminates.

That's it now,
abstract things have all fallen in pace.

I had the determination.
Now for your turn...
so now no need for crutches, no haze,
in one aspect, it's not the case and only,
but you are not inferior,
don't demean yourself,
but in a reference, or from a reference, or at a reference...
(not determined but done),

I am superior, that's the taste,
rather than the mediocre,
your taunts have resulted,
now I am a wholesome matter,
furthermore, imminent – greater than the greatest.

An Intresting New Year Journal Of 1-Jan-23

A new year's first day ended with an impromptu jog of 6 km at Carter Road.
Not the air resistance,
but...
small patches of the sprawling crowd on a New Year were a resistance,
and, thank God the dogs here are adapted to running people,
though all shackled with their owners,
but someone's two became unshackled and began to run...
as I ran at a pace.
I stopped; they stopped!
as they are only the epitome of the idiom said, "They know all the ill-minded people, thieves, and crucial culprits" needed to curtail.
 In a well-behaving human society,
and no doubt,
they are dedicated to caretaking that saying very gracefully,
I smiled at them, curtailed my tempo, and gave respect,
but didn't reflect their carefree owners,
what the heck :).
Here no one knows me in Mumbai, they may make a case,
at a point, one jumped onto me...
I covered my genitals in front gently as usual,
as I am a gender different than girls,
more afraid!!
but a few moments later... he confirmed that,
I was now hostile.
That was my style of encounter,
with a friendly taste.

Nocturnal And Diurnal Both She Is And Will Be Contagious… With All Days Not Even Excluding Me On Weekends Or Sundays

She is a girl… strong, but…
maybe a novice,
an inexperienced, but concluding himself as an expert can dent her reputation.
She is with me or not,
but she is, and will be of utmost importance and care.
A fallacy may come anytime,
I am likely to enjoy the feeling,
that she is inclined toward me,
if she feels ashamed!!
Of the misery of her soft heart!!
and that I am loquacious and talkative about her.

That's why when she began to show herself with someone else on Instagram,
to show that to me,
same words, same instances, same phrases…
you are not only special, I am like that,
I gauge.
That's why I proposed to her again with the full depth of my heart as my wisdom said…
as I am imploring, and I am a better beggar of her affection yesterday,

so that this moment may retain much more in her conscience and common sense,
than of the caress of her, whatever she pertained.
If done so and anyone humiliates her in my absence that - you are like that...
at everyone's in life has an open entrance.
She may become in a good stance rather than sensitive, much more normal.

By the way, I think we are not meeting each other,
on this small planet again.
So, that clinging and infectious as demanded side effects of her,
are with me including yesterday,
will play with my add-ons, with many more,
more specifically vivacious...
nocturnal and diurnal both,
she is and will be contagious,
with all days.
No, not even excluding me on weekends,
or on Sundays.

With my two hearts Candy and Bailey

Though with books, degree and certificates of being a writer, actor, fitness manager, master trainer, trainer for special populations, nutritionist, HIIT, TRX and Yoga instructor, State Gold Medalist and National Broze Medalist in Weightlifting too... and etc.

Rather than above,
I am happy that without having certificate from any academy or institution,
I have a "pet lover" designation too :)

The Slaughter House Becomes Gory

The Slaughterhouse becomes gory on demand of the gourmets.
Today is (Christmas/Holi/Eid), a fest,
so, excessively on the stones...
the chopping knives are being whet.

And here comes those poor broilers and fowls,
on the cheapest means arranged by the proprietor,
in throngs, congested.
Outside there are innards and other related internals and externals of things and belongings of their look-alikes...
they behold them for seconds,
and then felt qualm and thought that they were much better in the humane hands...
of the man who fed them timely...
(is absolutely not).

Because they don't have such or much of any thoughts...
in their pea-sized, meagre brains, and minds,
friends after all —
that's why they are fowls.
They simply saw the sight,
they don't even have censure for this mundane ritual,
because they don't have any idea related,
it's their first time experiencing and will be the last too...
and they don't even know!!
that after a few seconds or minutes, their eyes will experience an ultimate black spot.

It would be a human contemplation... that,
1)- Will they take birth again because the first life... spoiled... even before adolescence,
by those in vests with gory hands,
for their "vested interests."
2)- Or what is to happen that will happen...
being a martyr for others, is the most soothing...
self-assassination.
But rather than that —
actually because of lack of conscience...
they can't observe or recall these all,
and it seems like —
how cool are their gaits and their mindless confabulations.

(It's too a plus point... that emotions or senses both of them are not inflexed in them yet).
Suddenly a minion (of the proprietor) came up wobbly...
and without being attentive!!
grabbed the cages containing them,
from a lofty height,
and put them on the ground callously resulting in a thud sound...
that resulted in a stub of their toes,
and some blood began to ooze.

Time passed with nothing to do...
until a hand entered by unlocking the latches desperately,
and everyone ran by trampling each other senselessly,
nevertheless, he grabbed and snatched one easily.
Now this time — a surge ran throughout...
when the chirp-friendly left fowls began to experience mate's,
(who was doing frolics or jolting someone for space),
painful bawls excessively!!

After a while, that hand, handed over that fowl,
to a person who was normal and behaved fine...
he simply took his knife,
and with a "Ghaach" sound!!
beheaded him within no time.
The blood spurt out...
transcending the haphazard circle,
where he was reclined...
it too bespattered some areas and the red hue began to shine.
The body was fluttering beyond the examples,
the chirp which became something unearthly,
and in that condition (a pain which has no mercy),
he simply held his two legs in a plastic bin,
drained his red belongings,
until completely death... swooned life,
and tranquilized him with apart closed eyes.
Then he sheared,
minced that motionless body...
with nasty thuds of his chopping knife,
which instilled the fears,
and seeing something bestial atrocious too...
a man took up those in a black polythene (paid),
and for home from bench, he arose.

One or two of those —
those who haven't got senses still have the advantages.

{(Not only for billy-goats... cocks or hens, but if an atrocious thing is destined to happen...
and will happen... then sometimes —
emotionless people too... avoid and deliberately, inadvertently, or unknowingly averts,
much anguish and miseries,

than emotional wrecks and sensuals,
and sometimes unknown things,
until the finals...
are much pleasant (for the hens), and gives,
a soothing experience,
than knowing...
if it's ultimate that —
something unpleasant will happen)}.

By the way!!
But rest of all perspired,
they do understand at least what he is doing...
or happening over there,
is vehement and an unpleasant act,
and sweat ran down under those dense furs...
which no one observed...
(while observing these all through their steady gaze).

Everyone was petrified...
and the chaos and motion happened only when,
that disgusting hand came within different times.
One by one when assassinated, and the throng began to become less dense,
but just as a teacher on truancy, or on a clamorous shriek, or for other reasons...
in school thrashes every student found guilty,
from first row's first... to last row's last,
but the individual at last suffers more...
because time or duration, meanwhile,
does its play and gives immense excruciations.
Like respected Mithilesh sir is thrashing...
each student with his nasty look,
and with somehow arranged rigid broken crook,

and the one who suffered first is much lucky...
because he overcame much —
but the misery is for the last bencher's last student,
because with every second... and approaching sound,
his heart is going to burst.

By the way —
it was a joke only,
but just to contemplate and feel what happens,
when it would be...
or for the fowls, it is the ultimate verge of painful death.
If humans will experience the same for him,
or even a bit of this to his/her clans or brethren,
would he be so casual?

No - no!!
Rather than that they will watch belligerently even in fetters,
and will say... like in films,
"You will pay for your sins,
because God is watching our cries."

A child who was fond of his green parrot in his home,
gyrating for his non-veg momos in the evening...
by chance, first time observed this —
bestial savagery related to someone's life.
How can it ornate someone's plate!!
was his 1st thought...
and he sobbed a lot, rather than just cry.
A child is a child,
no matter what his religion is...
or aboriginal he is,
no matter that his ancestors were bestial hunters,
and he has latent antecedents...

or whether that is Salman Khan,
who will later change like the bulletins...
but every child, the first time in front of a butchery...
suffers a lot.
When the chirp of a bird becomes something unearthly...
and holy "Maa" calling animal...
turns into shreds and ugly flesh,
(that's the special trait of his).

Oh, Jesus!!
It's been long...!!
it's two thousand fifteen (2015),
and it's been long too...
after completing your life, you are up there!
See Almanac... please come,
as you said you will.
Disguise yourself as a son or a demigod or whatever excuse you can make...
and pamper that child because, according to the gospels,
as you said — he is your child.

Don't try to describe him in ways obscure,
it would be irrelevant,
if you will say my world only belongs to human beings,
not of those poor fowls,
but at least that time...
until he is childish and innocuous,
console him —
wipe his tears with your humane hands,
and just say... it's a part and circle of life.

{(He will later change, with the passage of time,
and then he will learn not to empathize,

and for his means, he will assassin even humans,
and would be worse than —
that man (afore-described),
who while seeing something bestial atrocious too... with someone's life...
he simply took up those in a black polythene,
paid... and for home from the bench, who arose)}.
(Meanwhile).

2 Years Old, Alan Kurdi Lying Dead On The Beach (2nd – Sept – 15) Iraq And Syria War

I have observed through my own eyes!!
that is...
not the origin of my own life...
but when I almost cried... everything was palpable,
but nothing I was able to ween and nothing I actually felt...
but in the present turbulent times...
forget about a decade, five years, a year, a month, or a fortnight,
friends! not even a single day is serene!
and not a single day passed when on the deeds of humans...
humanity didn't cry.

I searched on Google that stated that –
14 million children are impacted by conflict in Syria and Iraq...
some bodies of innocents below even 2 years are floating near the sea shore,
as the sea returned again, it seemed like...
the proofs are enough!
that there is absolutely no god, demigod, or any force divine.
The place where I am and from where I have searched (for security reasons) I won't describe.
Oh my god!!
those from top to bottom merciless black-clad abhorrent...
"means ISIS" guys!!

But above all... I have a belief,
that from the origin of this world,

as neither the violence is permanent nor temporary,
not the serenity is...
as neither the cruelty is constant, nor the generosity is...
and as two words come together and make an ultimate rhyme...
are War and Peace.
If War comes first then Peace comes next,
no matter what is going on or whatever would be amidst...
so, beyond the odds, we will survive...
and one day everything would be next to fine.

Because –
if someone in tyranny,
kills the violinist – so what???
if someone breaks the violin in pieces or three...
So what???
if someone would burn the notes so that no one would come to know that...
how the sound of harmony sounded actually,
so what???

Go tell them!!
then too if someone would assemble those pieces with fevi-kwik or stitches...
would put those strings on violin,
and would reform the glitches,
and would strum...
then too sound will come... depending on the efforts and that will not vary...
because a violin's sound was not murdered,
and that would be the sound of the same harmony which sounded...
and that would... with no imminent hazes...
again will enthral the life.

It's Their Obvious View

What — A *Tareef*, laud, applause or praise especially is?

Answer is simple — the thing or properties in which they are not so potent or adept,
but —
in front of them... you honed yourself up to that to achieve that, you were endowed with,
you are a prodigy, born talented, or whatever (that is nothing),
but only the person who is competent than them or is potent more than them,
at that point are you.

Have you ever noticed a child?
a child who does whatever as an instinct of his...
everyone beholds and notices him,
and says — Aaaa... lee... lee... puuchu... puuchu... how cute you are :),
he would sleep in deep sleep then too.

But after your childhood... the situation becomes different,
you are not selected individual to those who have garlands in their hands to hang around... the neck of yours,
remember you have the properties, qualities...
 which they don't have,
or you have achieved that, or you are able of the things,
or you are capable of doing those things...
what they can't do!!

Otherwise, if they could!!
they would prefer to wear those garlands themselves rather than you.

The simple thing is that —
mediocrity they have,
and how talented in front of them are you,
and remember when they will achieve that talent, mediocre are you.
So, work hard to achieve that,
Or if you have, then maintain it,
because... if you are not able to maintain that,
then they will become the teacher of you,
and will guide — this way, that way!!
O fool... why don't you??

No need to sit in the umbrage of a Bodhi tree and to meditate for weeks like Buddha...
to know that — what I am saying is it true...???

Very simple it is, in this present world,
 (if you have properties),
then it is the same as —
if you are a beautiful girl,
then only they are going to describe the beauty of you.

So, friends the point of view and conclusion is...
it's ok to be humble and thankful,
but nothing is much special in that,
it's their obvious view.

Sometimes Actually The Response Is Not Bad

Sometimes actually the response is not bad,
but the thing is —
people are unable to believe in you...
that the person whom they thought can do nothing or is good for nothing...
the same chap can do - such a fab.

And rather than to laud in public,
primarily —
in silence, they and their wisdom in apprehension likes to murmur mutually,
how could this be?
or on a miracle perceived, with their sealed lips they before blurting wow!!
remember!!
likes to utter instinctively —
WHAT WAS THAT!!

So, give them that shock regularly,
within the regular interval of time,
so that, they may believe in you,
but above all believe in yourself,
I would say,
that by your hard work...
on some day or the other,
(Whatever that was for you the conditions,
or they didn't stand for you),
but by your never-give-up attitude...

then too —
that underdog i.e., you (anyhow whatever be the condition), WILL BE THE CHAMP.
One day you will be exclusively you,
changing their points of view.

Vice Versa Conclusions

Everyone has faced untoward circumstances and situations.
Which later yielded the same...
"Lifeless feel" like conclusions,
and others confusingly consoled that —
"It was written... it was written."

Dejections and sorrows are common in every person's and individual's life,
somewhere everyone has groaned for their own related reasons,
just as every flower is pierced with a merciless needle if it is in a garland...
(or for instance, we are in life).
In a conclusion.

An anonymous observant sane said how eloquently that... "Life fucks all."
It's a lewd and bawdy retort while observing life, which he blurted...
but I must say it's the truth.

Life clamps and embraces all according to his whims and wills,
life never is serene for anyone,
when it never gives a sigh of relief to even,
a cot-friendly newborn baby!!
When he too bawls from his first second,
when he comes to experience Earth,
when he hasn't perceived even a bit,
and has nil of experience, conscience or sin...
then what are we??

So, don't be a grouch or grumpy person...
by facing it,
because you are not the only one,
vice versa...
if you are a weird thinker or your mind thinks weirdly,
then too —
you can't say that... life is biased,
while comparing yourself with someone...
and while observing his perennial-like smiles,
because maybe he is next —
 in (his/hers) hitlist,
to which it will behave more atrociously...
than... the cases whom even he or you had observed, or even seen.
(Sorry I have written his/her both because,
I am too a trainee still!!
I don't know too... actually that what exactly it is),
(male/female or middle).
By the way!!
so, be kind to a person (except in some exceptional cases),
and have some intentions to forgive a person...
who is a grouch up to a bit... behaves rudely,
or is grumpy.
(Don't retaliate),
because many a time he is nice by heart,
but as he has many trepidations and melancholy internally!
so, maybe it is possible or probably that due to that anxiety,
he is conveying to you his own false impression.

You can't crack his pate or skull to find out...
what is concealed,
and even in bonhomie...
no one can blab their own every time confidential,
so, who knows!!

from what anguish or miseries someone is suffering from???
That's why —
be pleasant to everyone and keep yourself calm,
because often it is unintentionally and inadvertently.

Friends!!
mind's behaviour is not like a carrion of carnivore, herbivore, or omnivore,
or whatever examples you may take,
(which is earthy),
which first doesn't smell...
but gradually with time, it gets lower,
a bit more... then higher,
and then an intolerable stench only!
until it completely decays or loses its own existence, with the curse of time.

Rather than that —
mind is a complex machine... it is fickle,
which changes its judgments, whims, and behaviours, with the passage of time...
if you don't believe!!
do analyse them or a particular person later...
give them time,
and you will find that again this time confronting you,
while going through duration or time's expedition...
he/she is a more attentive listener,
he/she is changed much,
and he/she has quenched, his/her anger, anxiety, and contorted face...
with a smile and too... a sorry expression.
And thus, you will find...
that life and its aura will be a better place to survive...
when there won't be a sulk instilled in your mind,

(because they were actually not insolent),
and everything would be next to fine...
DO TRY.

It starts from home...
the best example is our moms :),
but point to be noted...
with their ingenuity,
it may vary from person to person...
and life to life.

Life Is Not As Small As To Someone We Have To Write An Impressive Letter

No matter how much you are loaded with gyves and fetters,
and no matter how many and how austere the obstacles are which matters...
nevertheless!!
go... and fetch, own your aims, desires, and dreams,
and prove them —
how small actually they were.

Life is not as small as to someone we have to write an impressive letter,
it's a long journey...
so, don't be quite moody in choosing which moment you have to live...
and which you exactly abstractly don't want,
or you don't care.

Even in dejection and sorrows...
neglect your haplessness,
and live it enthusiastically because —
a tick of time too matters...
just as,
even every single brick is crucial to make a skyscraper.

Ornate it well...
belie those who say you can't.
People are those who will applaud...
and will or would increase your appetite,
but when you decline even haplessly,

most of them (above 97 in 100) will say things like,
son of William is much better...
or son of Natthu-Ram is fine.

So, don't rely on their bullshits...
on yourself and on only you,
in those days too of despair boy,
you have to rely.

If the sickle of disappointment is giving,
a dwarf look to the desires of yours...
and your confidence and morale are plummeting,
then too —
don't anticipate the upcoming depressingly...
do fight... with the conditions,
so that they may yield according to your desires and ambitions.

Hit hard the harsh bulks who say, they won't break!
and do notice their cracks meanwhile...
and prove to them too... that they were not weak,
but you were mightier from inside and outside,
solely and only, it was the trick.
Then —
every hard work of yours will...
will form blisters on your palm,
and they will slowly abrade your present misfortune's lines...
It will hurt a lot!!
but you will write your own destiny,
with newly grown new lines.
You will be successful by achieving those which for you and according to you...
defines, "Success."

So, go...
do nurture your present with your attitude...
by instilling those two famous three worded,
"Known slogan" but neglected sentences called:
Never give up,
and never say die.

And solemnly vow that —
you will not give up on your appetite or avidness...
just as a gluttony pigeon too... many a time gives up on grains,
with much advantages!!
but due to the burning of pan-like earthy ground...
and due to that scorching Sun.

Which shines.

And There You Are At 3:30 Am

It only occurs because of the friction due to...
the hesitant behaviour of mine,
and addiction of you when collides.

The intricate wiring of my mind abrades,
in every motion of your thoughts,
and becomes a reason for my insomnia,
and other more non-lucrative...
and non-legitimate symptoms and causes.

No matter how firm the doors are...
or looks,
if hinges or latches are weak.
Ushers are of a sense and conscience which are useless when I need them the most...
until someone may foray,
only recklessly they sleep.

Like a vagrant wind breaks all...
vice versa,
with a mild silence, you came...
and there you are at... 3:30 AM.
The thing for which I was unknowingly craved or craving for...
is now in front of me,
like a feeling, I am feeling it.
Now replacing those abundant unknown feelings with my tossing and turning,
as now there is glee.

My Dream Olympics

Mindset of mine towards... dreams of mine,
is not so infirm or weak,
that a small failure and someone will simply laugh...
or will smirk or grin,
and I will feel the guilt of seeing them.

That —
I will baulk,
only for the reasons that snide remarks of the known or unknown are
showing me the mirror,
and pretending about me that it's over...
and thus, in penitence, I will observe the loath for myself,
that when it was only a whim of my mind...
that conquered me and forced me to take those austere steps,
then why didn't I stop then?
and then known —
why I opted for less travelled or unknown fields... unlike them?
"No - No - Na - Na," I am not of that kind.

Because everything is on me.
Nothing is in their bullshit.
I won't frown at them,
neither I will consider their prognostications...
rather than that, I will rest —
until my time will come (in anguish) with their snides.

Because I haven't given up yet...
I still have faith and belief in my dream,
which I had dreamt...

I will cope with all the difficulties and miseries...
I will culminate one day and will find my zenith,
and that's the Olympics...
if I am a real dreamer and if that was not a reverie,
but a real dream of mine.
Because I know the potential, I still possess...
and too that —
the dice which I had thrown years back!!
while I gambled with myself and my life,
will yield the same,
and will obtain the same desired digits,
which I had desired... while taking my life at stake.
Because then too...
I was conscious that,
that was life, not an adventure sport of mine.

I will shun my practices of scribbling down the ideas,
that are the poems or poetry,
and I can bestow all those worthwhile emotional thoughts, and papers,
which I had jotted down under my pensive pen... into a flame!!
If I have to choose between, though both are unique, but...
this or that would become my mainstream.

Because this too... It's my hobby,
and an aspiration of (to be a bit of "Ghalib") may continue after youth...
but... an age of 37 or onwards, I think...
it will not be suited to this passion of mine...

Hitherto -
time was priceless which I had lost....
and will until left knee,
  ACL (Anterior Cruciate Ligament) surgery of mine!!

but as it's not a fiasco!!
and as —
nowadays a question is recurring and conquering me that:
What was my dream???
And where am I???
And as —
giving up is an option, but not an attitude of mine.

So, I will come back again and this time I will excel,
because this will be the final judgment,
that whether I would remain as a person...
that those smiling faces have instilled,
or will be that whom I had determined to achieve,
by giving the desired meaning to my life.

"Come what may,"
in the upcoming surges of fervours,
extraordinary will be the work or deed of mine,
which I will do from my side...
and thus, will bend my boat from shallow to where the fisheries are on a deeper side.

The Nicest Thing About Gymming, Weight Training Or Weightlifting Is The Moment

The nicest thing about Gymming, Weight-training, or Weight-Lifting...
is the moment...
when in peak exhaustion,
body says a big "No,"
but the mind still says a little "Yes,"
and the situation in between seems to look alike as a —
Roadways Bus is trapped in an unseen pit, due to huge rain... and its obvious weight,
on which,
engine generates sounds like —
"Vrooom... Vroom..." then black cloud of whatever it has in it,
even the stainless-steel pistons are burnt and by the process of sublimation they have to go,
it becomes the scene and their case.
Nevertheless, the only change in the whole story results in —
annoyed face of the driver... and the rotation of only rear-tires,
(but the bus remains the same).

Just as the body at its peak exhaustion... starts to tremble in pain,
but our muscular engine... needs more to lift the loaded weight...
but when anyhow, somehow!
the combining efforts of pain, shaking, brutally trembling engine, and sweat drops do that...
then that really small aim of a few seconds, achieved...
leads to say only one word for that so-called process of —
"Pain and Gain."

That's called —

"Awesome" :).
I did benevolence to myself,
what a taste.

It's His Problem

Every time I tried my best...
so that, my eyes may soak all the tear particle,
that oozes out in the memories of you.

Girl,
by rotating my eyes left and right,
and by adjusting my pensive head,
filled with those thoughts of you,
but then too... though of the hindrance offered!
they spill and embarrass me.

My eyes have numerously expelled these tears in pain,
whatever the ambiances were...
the above is only an instance disclosed,
if you are reading it...
in a busy and so-called tedious schedule of yours.

I thought about the time I in which I am missing and feeling
incomplete without you...
will pass like a whim of someone for something,
but unfortunately!!
you are as you were, a long time ago in me,
as you were on an unknown date,
on September–October past year,
when I was lost in your thoughts...
even inadvertently, you have hurt me...
this time again with a different emotional hue.

My heart was blissful... so was I, in the company of you...

but the contusions that you gave to my heart... affected him so much,
that now he beats only to support my life,
and nothing is there to boast of,
that I have a bit of mirth bliss...
or I am alive!!

Girl, I cannot describe...
that why a meaningless thing,
still means and matters to me,
and why in every moment of mine,
there is an influence of you,
and if I did that too... then too I know!
neither my feelings would touch your heart,
and nor you would know the depth of my emotions,
that are there for you,
because sorry!!
a person who is in love,
may understand the dilemma in me,
but you are not in it anymore...
and only for my own inclination —
another reason is... I don't want to entice you.

Girl, you don't have even a single rue!!
I was unaware of this fact!!
I thought despair due to distances between us, is just as the distance between us...
until a close friend of mine and yours,
told me two days ago, that you are happy that you hurt me... that's not all!!
but you said, "It's his problem if he still loves me."
And I am apprehensive, musing since that...
whom I know and who were you!!

And on this note, I just want to say that...
I never knew!
I swear... I was unknown!
that, time which I had with you,
will not forgive my present,
otherwise!!
I could have neglected you,
and thus, could have averted the reason for each and every pain present,
what I got from you,
because pain becomes worse...
and every bit of that affects more and behaves atrociously...
when someone close gives it to you,
and Girl,
I experienced it unfortunately, only because in my heart there was a special room for you...
and if yesterday I cried, then still more than a bit,
I have enough for you.

I Am Still Fiend Of You

It was easy to fall in love with you,
but even if it's hard to continue —
then too I will do.

I will not ever say something just to simplify the conditions for me,
because I'm too keen to know,
that —
if I had ever loved you truly,
and if my heart that throbbed for you ever,
then in what conditions and in what miseries,
without observing even, a single regret —
I can love to love you.

Girl, now!!
thoughts related to you, which hurt me,
 are too familiar and friendly too...
they don't pester me actually,
and as,
there were enormous reasons to love you,
so, there will always be at least one.

You dear, continue on!!
in the worst cases too...
I won't tell you that for which one reason,
I'm loving you...
and for whom —
I'm still fiend of you.

Sorry, Don't Mind 😊

In life, for a reason big or small!
if someone, whether that's a gentleman,
a woman for whom you have fantasies...
and whose presence in front of you,
instils a fear that...
does she know or not!!
or your dream girl...
or even for instance —
whenever, wherever's real Shakira,
(applause you).

Sorry, don't mind :)
but all I want to say is...
every person mattering from (very to little),
if they applaud you!!
then too, friends!!
it's ok to be humble,
and then you can mumble some words like —
"Thanks," and all that...
but for it, don't ever commit suicide...
in an immense rapture or elation from a cliff,
that they have applauded!!
and again, I will say —
somehow try to behave like it's okay,
because remember!!
albeit they have applauded,
but it's too true that —
something in you is or was praiseworthy,
you have done that immense assiduity,

you toiled like a donkey,
in every tedious and austere conditions,
and then they have opted to clap,
or to utter good, well, or excellent confabs.

And common '*yaar*'...!!
when someone will do better than you,
as you have done the same,
then they will clap for him or her,
and suddenly, haplessly, you will become —
only a nerd nonentity for them,
because —
nothing is serious in this matter,
and nor is it special...
that's simply human nature.

Sorry, I Was Inept To Find It

It has been long,
and it's a thing in the past for you dear!!
but from dawns to dusks...
then dusks to dawns,
from days to months,
and then from months to years... and all that,
I'm still obsessed with the thoughts that —
had you ever read all the emotions related to you,
that lied to you!!
but factually lay in my eyes??

I thought I knew you well...!!
but like a riddle which has its own latent meaning within,
you were the same,
what you wanted...
sorry, I was inept to find it,
and that was sheer fault of mine...
and maybe that's why you became so ruthless,
and in return, in caprice, because of you...
I left my passion for life,
but what was the incantation done by you,
say, Girl!!
that I don't know why you forgot,
every bit but till date,
I am assailable and weak when it comes to you,
and so, for this very reason!!
your memories and related emotions,
assails me from time to time.

You were always ornated well by my heart...
even in my reveries,
and you are still —
like a tulip with its scent and fragrance,
without the factor or ambits of time.

You are happy, that's the happiest thing for me,
and too...
a broken thing in me still respects you,
for the choices you made...
but one should beat me, lash me,
as per the ill rituals of being fine,
for the statement which I'm going to state that...
as it is a gospel truth,
that Sun has its existence in the sky!!
I still feel everything for you,
whether you belong to someone else,
and every second,
every feeling takes something out of me (that's life),
and don't know why like an insane,
my eyes without a blink,
stares at the horizon...
and think that do they actually meet???
and meanwhile, a tear slithers from the corners of my eyes,
and asks — my beloved!!
Will you ever be mine???

I Have Blinkers On My Eyes

How will you descend or decline from the position,
to which my heart has entitled you, beloved!!
if you would try to do that by your insolent behaviour or whatever!!
then too... my heart will feel the elapsed time with you,
and then again by omitting all,
it will again fall in love with the person you were.

By the way!!
now I'm habitual to the pain given,
it's ok,
that's why —
my anguish won't retort or will blurt,
a single word for you.
Just feel it like —
I have blinkers on my eyes,
and thus, I can see only the goodness in you,
 Girl!!
and the rest of the whole is restricted,
by my own conscience when it comes to you,
and the worst part for me and best for you is...
if complete breakup will happen!!
then too!!
your position is safe and secure in my heart,
and will always be.
I'm not so fickle,
that I will think or love someone else!!
instead of you.

Albeit then too you won't be mine... I know,
but...
a smile would never fade away,
that I met a person in my life,
like you...
you might not be the most beautiful person,
nor am I in this world, or even in the district or in the state,
but you were increasing rapidly like to be a nymph,
as my love was increasing for you,
and I promise I will continue.
If I am falling, in the reverse conditions too...
and will see how much my love was true,
without promising, I promise...
like a thing is of the colour, which it reflects,
absorbing all...
I will seek only for the indulgence and inclination of you.

With My Utmost Conscience, I Am In A Dim Sense Or An Innocent View

At which moment, time, or when I got involved,
with my heart admiring you...
I don't even know.

Maybe the time which I had with you,
attracted me as hell like an indulgence for a desired thing unknowingly,
when I suddenly felt alone without you.
I know things now are much changed,
and somewhere I too accept that...
with my utmost conscience and immense pain.
But nevertheless, I don't know why!!
like an instinct uncontrolled —
I can't curb my desire to be with you.

Every decency of yours, still insists me to explore you even more in my memories,
and then resulting in —
unusual ruining of unexpected time on you.
I fortified myself as much as I could,
and defended myself by not going into a reminiscent mood...
but your thoughts besiege me everywhere,
and thus, as I never had neglected you.
I in me...
never came out with a statement that,
with the passage of time, if for you and in you,
today I'm nothing —
then as the same,

I too have to disown you and achieve that same state of mind,
simply as you did it too.

On going through a bit of those conditions "to degrade you,"
it seems like —
what would I achieve by erasing you???
what would be the life in me —
without a hovering beautiful thought of you.
Then comes another that —
when my heart won't bear a pain related!!
then how would I know?
that every moment with you was true...
and in it,
every bit of that was an incomparable elation,
which you did like a benevolence to me,
for whom I am indebted still to you...
and if ultimately, I would neglect the feelings in me related to you,
then how would I experience the experiences that...
in my life, I too can love someone,
with such an insane intensity...
and with such low probability!!
no matter what or whether for you or someone,
that's a dim sense...
or rather that's an innocent view.

I know I'm a fool and it's precarious that...
will my feelings be accepted or neglected by you!!
but as in those pains and pangs, I can feel you...
so, I opt always and every time to be in pain,
because in that immense pain and in those tears...
I can most get the feel of you.

I know things are much different and I have accepted it too...

but whether or what would be the fate of mine,
I won't overcome it because I don't want to.

It won't affect you; I think...
but nevertheless, like a sin committed by me,
after the cremation of my desires,
I will burn like a burnt thing innocently and repeatedly...
while remaining the same black hue,
and thus ultimately, I think,
I will pay the immense cost of loving you.

An Experience Which Usually Increases

An experience which usually increases,
and as much I have experienced,
that much is enough for me.

That I won't forget you!!

Limited were the moments with you,
but in those —
surplus were the emotions and today...
surplus is the pain,
which is still in me,
and on feeling, it feels as if...
a broken thing in me is still beating for you.

Girl!!
every emotion has its own class and a related crazy view,
and today I wanna confess it to you...
in my fantasy related to you,
when combined with true desires,
it migrates me to the feeling that —
one day you will be mine...
and for that day, I wanna strive and crave,
because... on feeling... at every moment or in caprice,
it feels great!!
like a pleasant thing with its pleasant view.

Maybe it is all because...
I am not so wise for the facts that,

I cannot taste a new taste as the lechers do...
but despite the fact I am happy because —
I am proving that,
I am an emotional fool for you...
and a true lover of yours,
and by seeing a percent of possibility!!
I am bounded with the emotions,
by remembering that...
you belonged to me,
and I belong to you,
and I won't give even an inch of place in my heart,
to someone except you.

Because I will wait... I will wait... I will wait...
only and only for you,
and even in my soul,
my soulmate,
I miss you.

Upto An Aeon You Will Always Be Precious To Me Just As Feeling For Life And Scars To Realize

Like the brims or fringes of river have mixed feelings of wetness and dryness,
I too feel the same with a wetness in my eyes,
and a compromising smile.

Sage says that!!
"Nothing is permanent in this world."
But I promise and internally my heart agrees,
that the emotions for a person like you...
will permanently remain in me until my demise.

Girl, I don't believe in rebirths,
and I don't believe in those hecks called eternity.
Despite that, I'm quite interested in the scheme of memorizing you,
up to an eon!!
and thus, ruining mine single so-called...
God's gifted life.
There is no logical meter available or yet invented,
which can measure the pain in me related to you,
but despite that my grimace or my pouted face,
will never blame —
for what I'm suffering from...
I promise,
because —
if I did that...
then I would be remiss by forgetting that countless moments,

when with the involvement of yours...
my lips have experienced the meaning of a true lively smile,
which were too die-hard dreams of mine,
If I get with the involvement of you... I still remember, what kind of urge it was!
once upon a time.
And ultimately, I want to say that!!
there is no coercion from me or my side,
that you have to and have to feel me and...
all those belongings which were about,
you lamented or not on the situations of mine,
due to you...
or just dodged it internally as a meaningless thing —
it too doesn't matter to me,
but besides these questions —
as an instinct in me, I will unconditionally love you...
you will always be precious to me...
just as —
feelings for life and scars to realize...
it's understood —
like a guarantee on some product,
you didn't come obviously to me...
like giving a customer,
only a satisfactory smile.

Nevertheless

Tragic thing happened to me that you forgot me!!
but why should I take a stance to erase you???

Time is a live thing that is going on...
and you are a gone thing, unfortunately.
Nevertheless!!
my heart enjoys the causes,
that you were a memorable thing still dwelling on.

A girl is not the ultimate thing that makes life,
I know my heart will definitely belie...
because still, with a single memory of yours,
he with me without getting bored,
can wander miles and miles.

But many a time I too ponder about the familiar facts that —
the things that existed between us matter to me,
every second of my life...
because those causes were necessary,
somewhere today as an inspiration to write a rhyme.
Then being highly obliged to you,
I'm generalizing that...
besides the pangs that you gave me,
which drenches my eyes from time to time.
Ooh... yes... definitely and doubtlessly!!

You were indeed a nice thing, happened to my life.

I Can Demean Me, In Myself

I am quite depressed by the attitude of mine toward you,
because every sense of mine becomes senseless when my heart starts admiring you.

I won't forget you!!
because somewhere in me I don't want to!!
You emerged well... on which I don't have any issues related to beloved!!
but please don't prove that —
a painful thing, was being with you!!
by smiling on the sentiments which you had!!
but in me,
if those bullshits are still unfortunately capable to squeeze all those emotion-laden tears...
which are still attached,
as an immense guilt of loving you.
Many a time, not in me who loves you immensely,
but my subconscious mind may take any of the random fractions sarcastically,
and can demean me in myself...
 with its own crafted story and averse reverse spectacle view,
and I may have to hate myself,
as I am not inculcated...
or,
as I am not in practice or even in the initiation of hating you,
don't share the private words of reverence...
in your circle,
which are now without a connection,
and now are no doubt ludicrous to you!

because I don't do it in my circle too...
otherwise, how did I come to know the connotation or hint of,
what I shared mutually only with you?
many or a bit of other scribbles which were private!
but say —
like the accent of my in the nicknames of you...
it hurts me true.

The Connection, The Vibes, The Anecdotes And My Internal State

The connection, the vibe, the anecdotes,
all mesmerizing... have a state of their own in my brain...
that still when hums in me,
causes stillness of my gait.
Whatever the task to perform,
all become oblivious except you,
because I think immense concentration is needed to receive...
whatever was perceived of you.

You never meant to harass me,
but Girl, internally your memory does...
it's true!
it's career-making time and I am without any cloy,
submerged in you.

I fought as much as I could... and then,
time too... has evolved me that much...
but nevertheless!!
a proportion of everything to nothing lies in my internal state...
don't know but absolutely needed to express,
only to you in the sense that, Girl —
you neglected me and ultimately,
one day...
I have to show you that...
internally, I loved you and cared for you, dear,
how much!
I swear I will write a book on you...
and see in your hands you are reading a published and renowned poet!
who has literally written poems on you.

When You Were Not A Mistress Of An Unfortunate Pea-Sized Brain

Every time I approached you...
and denied too!!
The thoughts murmured...
and deferred themselves too!!

You judged me, by my behaviour,
And I do too...
I think I behaved like the symptoms too!!
I meant all...
behind my concealed gestures, Girl!!
and I too observed and felt...
those biased heart-related feelings for me,
in you!!
but even though, the fact that...
I never confab about them to you...
no anomaly,
like you did too...
for God's sake!!
just answer one thing for me, that...
for these remorse and sufferings,
which I am experiencing in my present days,
and in my daily life!
due to you...
were those "three words untold" are the only offense I did?
when you were not a mistress of...
an unfortunate pea-sized brain!!
and when totally,
you were capable of realizing my complete sentiments,

and my polite hesitant behaviour...
which resided in me,
only for you????
and said silently that not any inclination or liking,
but I love you.

Say Girl say... from whatever source you want to...
say Girl say... from whatever source you want to.

You Should Know Girl, From Then You Will Only Become An Evanescent Material In Me

No one told me... and even I hadn't observed that,
the time which I am elapsing with you...
would be a memorable torment for me,
and will give the pangs of a lifetime to me.

Maybe today my eyes have started diminishing the quantities of my tears,
maybe because, it has been long...
and they are quite used up too!!
and can handle my emotions well.

But you should know, Girl!!
that the pain which abides with me till today is still the same,
because —
my heart always generalizes that,
you were not supposed to do, what you did...
and the done things and all those pieces of stuff were done inadvertently to me.

Otherwise!!
internally about me, you know that,
and I too feel that, if I am determined by something, Girl...
then I'm sure that I can achieve it,
and from then, you will only become an evanescent material in me,
but because of the aforesaid generalizations of my heart...
and the unfortunate retentiveness in me,

the soft caring nature for you in me,
time never forgave me...
for the impressions which you had left on me,
and it seems like —
every sorrow has its own beauty when it relates me to you.

That's why actually it doesn't feel to me,
and it's not important to peep that,
in your eyes there lies an image of mine or not!!
but in me, it gives a sense of satisfaction that...!!
I haven't omitted even a thing about you,
and in my eyes if a tear feels something for you...
and then falls from the brims!!
then there lies an indication,
that there lies an immensely cute feeling about you...
on which note I loved you,
which still makes a moment for me,
for those a bit to immense, I am indebted to you.

You Cannot By Your Present Phase Overwrite Me

Sometimes it seems like I am living life!!
but I'm absolutely unable to feel it,
every innocence of yours cajoles me...
and murders the sulk,
which resides in me for you...
even then —
your every moment with me...
gestures...
behaviours...
anecdotes...
behave like a documentary recorded!!
and don't know why!!
I enjoy them thoroughly,
when my mind still plays them all...
and my heart still beats for those,
everywhere, every time immensely...
on the memories already performed,
and then, Girl!!
by judging you by those aspects —
my heart forgives you for the reasons,
by generalizing the conclusion that...
anything can change, even you,
with time!!
but it's impossible, even for you,
to change the incense of yours...
in my memories.

That's it... examples will fill page after page making a book of itself,
but the conclusion is and will be...
you cannot by your present, overwrite me,
because the present ink is very dilute,
to have its own mark or impression on the past,
believe me.

Maturity Is Not Suiting You

After many days... I think six or seven days,
I found myself there again —
I was engaged in the memories of you!!

Every aspect of you, again mesmerized me...
of those dramatic encounters with you,
and then the exchanges of those fortunate gazes!!
my mind then continued the mimicry of my voices which I pronounced for you...
and you too then completed your own phrases!!
then —
don't know why, and by what sentimental norms!!
me and especially my two eyes got rewarded by those glittery teary hazes,
after that —
I chuckled even more internally!!
and experienced that I tried my level best,
but the deliverance from you in me,
it is not so easy...
because the pain given by you is closer to approximately nothing,
when compared to the innocence in you, that lay within you...
inadvertently those days,
in your adolescent ages,
(maturity is not suiting you).
I am not going to tell you frankly this type of sentences and phrases,
as you are eliminating me or have eliminated me slowly-slowly from that proximity!
and at first sight too...
it seems like I cannot do even a sentence of this kind,

even a jot of whatever will become audacity to you...
and my heart is thinking rigorously,
what kind of nonsense to all the talks we shared!!
and where we are now...
where are you!!

You Are My Olympic Medal For Lifetime Girl

I will never forget you... just as,
time doesn't ever forget the history*,
deep scars don't lose their symbolic taints,
and, Girl!!
just as gores too...
never forget to attain a partial swell,
as for example —
which I experienced severely by undergoing that heck!!
Anterior Cruciate Ligament (ACL) injury in my left knee accidently.
After being operated,
still, there is a fire of winning an Olympic medal for my country,
for Weightlifting Sports, no grudges...
even for the crutches.

By the way... same as!!
you will continue to dwell in me, as...
the ultimate consequences :).
Then too...
if it will be giving me a hindrance or a slow pace,
I swear!!
I will always embrace you in my memories...
it's not true...
but —
through reverence,
I will win you one day,
whatever you will do.
Here too ultimately after winning you,
no grudges.

Winning you for a lifetime somehow, anyhow...
Is lifetime continuation of Olympic medals.

Girl, You Were Impeccable, I Accept

I'm wretched only by the circumstances and situations.

Like a beheaded body!!
who experienced the death,
but by the grace of yours,
the sword used was of "stainless-steel" for his assassination.

From the rummage of thoughts and all the thoughts,
my heart only accepts the good ones,
and dwells on it... till one tear slithers,
and describes that it was too... a painful description.

Girl, you were impeccable... I accept...
but you never understood that,
hailstones fall from the sky,
and accumulate themselves on the ground...
but —
from the same source... sunlight,
don't have such illustrations!!
because —
everyone has their own properties in their own proportions.

And that's why... you nitpicked well.
I sobbed a lot, but meanwhile, you left me,
I too, in the deduced caprice of self-esteem,
without showing you that you were a bit wrong,
and I can too... change myself,
so too... your personal investigations.

I in front gave not so much of aligned reactions.

But lastly and eventually!!
as a ritual of true love without you...
and as I afore said that I was wretched!!

Everything affected me!!
just as each day affects life,
and yet till today —
only because of you...
I have a lifeless feeling,
by rather than God's,
someone's reverse grace,
in all my lively and... trendy seasons.

And in the continuum, that's the continuous conclusion.

18th Feb.

It's not Valentine's Day, 14th Feb... so what???
It's the 15th... So what???

Today I'm a frivolous trash for you!!
but Girl :(,
I have registered genuine pages in the tome,
or you may simply say in the book of my love life,
which I had with you...
in which —
fascinating are the facts...
which are prominent too,
and states that!!
my heart was not so biased... just for the reasons only, that I loved you,
but in spite of that!!
your caress has many more described moments that disclose,
that when and at what moment...
I experienced the true love that dwelled for me so sincerely in you.
That's why Girl!!
maybe I am an impudent today,
but for those moments!!
and to believe you, that I too loved you truly... in which I lacked,
and so, to judge... it's the same you (that was),
I won't give up... so easily in this gory battle if someone comes in to intervene...
everything is acceptable for you :).

Remember —
in spite of the contusions that you gave to my heart...
nevertheless!!

in the Tunes of Time
I will wait... I will wait.
Just as the poets say, "Till the last breath,"
"only" to enhance the effect of their poetry on the reading clans.
Same as Beloved!!
reverse of that...
I really mean it,
I will genuinely continue the play of life for you.

In spite of painful belongings related to you,
like a latent soothing play,
I will genuinely continue the play of life for you.

It's Not Coincidently But Conditionally

Many times, really... I don't enjoy the praise of someone,
because someone praises you only when,
something is praiseworthy!!

It's not coincidently but conditionally,
on your deeds...
because —
there are glees, when everyone supports and cheers... for your deeds,
what you did,
and there are flaws...
when everyone neglects you,
and suddenly you are accused of ineligibility.

So, it's the greatness of you,
when someone really entitles you, as great!
and when you are not... no one bothers, you become nonentity.

Harsh but true,
nothing else... that's it,
it's the reality.

I Am Anonymous For You
It's The Accepted Truth To Me

1)- In this mean world...
   if someone has an abundance of something,
   nevertheless...
   some people give nothing, even a bit of that, willingly.

2)- And some inadvertently!!
    gives the memories and emotions,
      which resides and remains without the factor of duration or time.

You were the one, Girl!!
of course, the second type.
In the inebriation of your thoughts...
my heart strays from the feeling of life,
I recovered as much as I could...
but till yet —
before my revival,
every moment strangles me for the lost moments,
which I had with you when you were mine.

One day doesn't matter to me...
whether it's special or what... Valentine's!!
when your pain and especially you dwell in me,
every and each second of my life.

I am an anonymous for you... it's the accepted truth for me,
and too I'm trying to disown you, with the same factor of time,
but hardly, don't know why!!
I feel I'm really little bit happy for the reason,

that like a habit or hobby —
my heart throbs for you like someone's for life.

And above all!!
my mind enjoys the time-pass discussions...
and till yet —
all those which are not deducible... Introspections about you,
which gives a cute,
but meaningless smile :)

Which is too... a worthwhile.

But In The Religion Of Love
I Actually And Absolutely Revered
You

My heart celebrates the loneliness it has,
with the memories of you.

It has been long...
but the fact that I can't forget you,
is ultimate and true.

You are a personal thing to me,
like a thought of someone's
that's why...
even you don't own a right to say,
before my demise, I have to erase you.
Like a flower blooms and wilts!!
obliviously, even my soul, I think...
enjoy the past bloomed phase of mine with you.

I loved you, not a bit —
but in the religion of love, I actually and absolutely revered you.
Girl!!
countless are the emotions given by you to me,
because —
countless were the moments which I elapsed by feeling you... with you.

That's why!!
it occasionally becomes a torment for me,

when I realize in my conscious mind that even after the immense pain that you gave me,
my heart is still beating for you,
but the rest of the time!!
In solitude, I enjoy the feeling that no matter what you feel... today for me!!
but I'm still unexpectedly continuing the emotions of a recognized and a good-hearted person,
heartily still known to me, in every hazy situation of my life...
who resides in me by the name of you,
or maybe if investigated that is,

absolutely you.

The Wetness In My Eyes Is The Witness That I'm Feeling You

The duration of time doesn't matter to me...
from when you left me,
the duration of time mattered,
when I was with you.

My eyes get drenched in pain and sufferance,
just as!!
if poured from the former bucket to another even whole,
the next dwelling bucket (of a painter), always innocently misses some of its hue,
beyond the capacity as they are still especially special,
and in my own verdict, they have occupied too much space,
as I can't leave them, that's why I am congested, reason being...
they all have some soothing essence of you.
Same as!!
the excruciations of mine which belong to you,
becomes beyond the limits,
when I feel —
that in my present days,
my present time is too...
losing an unexpected time in you.

Yes, I do believe...
you were a culprit, Girl!
for giving me those momentous emotions and memories of you,
that's why today!!
even after many introspections and heartiest tries by me,
as a victim...

I am quite busy with the reasons why I should love you???
because I have quite less reasonable reasons,
that why should I hate you???

And at last, at the end of the day!!
with every forward step in my life,
I feel that,
the wetness in my eyes, is the witness that I'm feeling you.

And yup... I'm still fond of the emotions that are related to you...
and in front of an idol, whether it's Narsimha or Hanuman or Durga...
whoever it is, even Allah... if I'm praying,
even after years in my prayers,
I am mentioning you...
and sending blessings, prayers, and supplications to you.

You are not a termite, but...
beautifully you may say,
I am infested by you.

I Am Knocking At The Door Delicately Of Your Heart So, That It Will Feel You But Won't Hurt You

I never did forget you.

My heart is still a patron of all my emotions,
related to you.

On memorizing you,
I feel like I'm still burning alive,
without a single retorted word,
and not even a facial hue.
In penance!!
tears accumulate themselves expressively,
and then fall from the brims of my eyes,
just as!!
they too project that they are committing suicide from a height,
because by feeling that the elation and joy don't matter to them,
whatever the source is...
rather than that!!
they just and just want a true time in the company of you.

Really Girl!!
I am knocking at the door...
delicately of your heart,
so that you will feel it, but it won't hurt you.

And I'm saying to you that...
I'm sorry!!
Whatever the sacrifice, I did externally...
and kept on ignoring you,
but internally!!
the conclusion is still the same.... and annoying,
that in my soul...
immensely and immensely...
my soulmate,
"I still love you."

Absurd Poetry But Not On Love

In the fuss of day-to-day life...
1)- Whenever you are soft, silly...
    people assume you a fool,
      or in Hindi *Chu##ya*.

Alike,
a stagnant pole on the nook of a roadside...
on whose posture every dog wants to pee.

On the same standard dilemma,
when someone wants to pee...
and —
2)- When jolted or retorted.
    If he would say — nowadays this attitude!!
    days would bring, don't know what much...
    when you would be the wannabe!!

Woooo... woooo... woooo... hold on, hold on, dear!!
In this context and in this scenario...
and due to that, it's not that... I would say enough is enough,
I want to bring it to your kind notice that,
between my attitude and between being a *chu##ya*.

There is always a middle way, where you actually deserve to be,
or you may assume it like in slang, a middle finger penetrating your Stayfree.

In between you may go into your reminiscent mood and through the rummage of...

retained mental records and when investigations are done,
observe that...
I just acted or represented the same obvious way,
where you didn't mind behaving to me,
and due to that, it's not that...
I would say – enough is enough, "Respect me."
"Respected Sir", "Respect me."
But in one trial now my mood is giving you a warning like a caption displayed firmly,
in short, being liable for your health and wellness,
remember those four sane words that, — "DON'T MESS WITH ME."

Otherwise, you would finally and really end up realizing that...
a middle finger penetrating your Stayfree.

Because remember,
finally dear, I am not that kind of person,
I am supposed to be,
so, in your full consciousness, and even nightmares too...
don't clash with me.

Because You Were Not A Short-Lived Desire Of Mine

You may be of someone else...
but up to eternity, you will be mine.

You were the scarlet-coloured rose in the garden of my life,
and will be without changing, throughout the span of my life.

The effect of time, tides, and vagrant winds will not be able to fade and wilt every aspect
and particular of those things for which you are revered and will be revered in me.

Your beauty and youth are none of them...
because you were not a short-lived desire of mine.

See

See what I can do with minimal you,
the proud moment is this...

not how much I got you.

5 Points Why Should I Select You

1)- I HAVE KNOWLEDGE TO APPLY.
2)- PASSION FOR WHAT I LIKE,
WISDOM TO SUFFICE.
3)- DEVOTION AND DEDICATION FOR MY WORK ARE ALIKE.
4)- LIKE AN INSTINCT TO SURVIVE –
MODERATION THAN BINGE, IS A HABIT OF MINE.

AND SIR,
5)- CONFIDENCE AND IMAGINATIONS IN ME ARE IN A SUCH PLANNED MANNER THAT,
 I CAN CULMINATE ONE DAY AND CAN ACTUALLY FIND THE ZENITH JUST AS THAT WAS DESTINED AND DECLARED FOR ME TO BE GIVEN...

BUT AT A PARTICULAR TIME.

Created in some minutes for an interview on frequently asked questions like
 "Give us five points what's in you...
or five points why should we select you."

So Many Slogans On Aim

If to attain or to achieve even a bit of,
any mind-picked wish was...
so, easy, simple, crisp, and both up and down smooth.

Then to boost the morale,
there wouldn't have been...
so many slogans on aims,
and in front of a deity,
there were not much people questioning, saluting, and begging,
that how to be in the process...
and how to overcome the incurring process of pains.

So, test the difficulties,
never give up...
and profusely thus enjoy the gains,
averse reverse whatever!
take inspiration from...
even in a pan and with a spatula,
 you are making hurricanes.

A Single Life

A "Single Life"!!
spared on security and not taken on risk,
is just like...
a melded iron, not hammered for an experiment,
and left as a lump of...
a meaningless... and unidentified structural object.

Failure

Failure is just an enthusiasm aggravated for the next time...
some more and more,
brutality on myself,
and my success with me for a lifetime engaged.

A Curved Path May Delay

A curved path may delay!!
but we should never diminish the excitement of being there,
to which we were determined of.

Just as waves of the sea!!
fighting with the uneven slopes in her path,
and just as she too...
returns back only when,
she attains and feels the touch of the last sand particle...
to which she was determined for.

Everyone Makes His Meal On Fire

Everyone makes his meal on fire...
then after this, without thanking him,
tastes its calmness and sleeps.

And until it burns the life of someone...
they really —
never feel the dangerousness of it.

Sometimes modesty really belongs to it.

I Was But Sorry

I was!!

But from now on... I am not hungry for the admiration of the people,
because failures of life have taught me,
that why they admire,
and why they don't!!

So,
if I am bald in the middle of my head,
then I am not gonna hide it with a wig,
in a belief...
that they will feel good or comfortable for it.

But instead of that —
I would insist them to admire the,
hairy pussy of a whore!!
if it can give them,
some pleasure too.

And let my bald (head) prone to shine.

Hey Vishal!!

When someone assumes I am a fool...
and absolutely fucks the delicacy of my heart,
and it seems like a curse to be so emotional!!

Then the evaporation of my mind internally becomes,
just like an evaporating steam that blurs...
and gives a translucent scene to the winds.

But of course, that person can't see that,
on observing it with an eyesight.
Nevertheless, he continues ruining my mood and mind,
just as a lemon being crushed under tires...
in preparation for an unusual ceremony,
of being fine.

Then particle-to-particle of mine says to me...
that, "Come what may!!"
but fuck him the same way too.

And, in that commences, my friends!!
when my organ begins to enhance his size in my own underwear,
and ultimately when...
my emotional-victim heart blinks his eyes,
and stares upward in the usual confidence,
in a while...
and in shock, when I observe a shocking sentence by him...
accenting that...
"Hey Vishal!!
that motherfucker is gone!!"

then my whole body feels so dizzy :).

And it becomes only a grace to him...
that after a day or two,
I too forget him and his deeds...
assuming that I was the useless hyper,
he was just a murmuring drunk,
no clashes in business from either side.

Like The Rain Drops Are Always Tangent To Their Sky

Even in every happiness,
my heart seeks the sadness related to you,
and on that!!
like a freak,
without expecting an answer in return,
I too seldom,
and usually ask my questions to you:
That —
Why your memory is like a shadow in me?
which doesn't fade itself...
with the factor of day and night?
and why??
if you were only a glimpse of time,
in my life...
then why are you in me still,
like the raindrops are...
always tangents to their sky.

Even in casual behavior...
a beggar doesn't seem like, he is begging for.

But when he uplifts his hands...
and wears a sadness on his face,
then he totally seems like!!

And this too seems like that Girl!!
you won't understand the dilemma of my emotions... in seemingly normal behavior too!!

So, say!!
how should I bow in front of you?
to ask the fees!!
in return for your past love?

Which was a synonym for me,
 of my life-like.

Thank You

I desired you,
and I got,
an undesired amount of pain from you.

Girl, it seemed like!!
a caption was too... given to me by you...
that —
an unwanted word too... doesn't deserve its meaning,
in a meaningful sentence...
written by you.

The "Decibel" Of Sound

I never announced the pain in me,
the "decibel" of sound...
which penetrated the silence in me.

In fact!!
I had a briefcase of sadness...
whose weight solely,
and only bothered me.

And too... Girl!!
internally a carpet of the color red was also floored by me,
in an intention that!!
may the heart's blood of mine, get match to it,
and the translation of pain,
and too... the brutality of you,
rather than others...
as it is belonging,
should also...
may only remain into me.

The Water Of Washed-Off Clothes

The water of washed-off clothes!!
cannot be the same in purity,
as the fresh one!!

And it's too a victory for you, Girl!!
that my true love was wasted on you,
hasn't the guts too...
till today,
to even get prepared for another one,
as in that context too, you lost some colour of yours and materials in me,
and now,
just as I am inferior and would be in a pang of guilt until my lifetime,
for losing my purity,
maybe now no one other for me.

The Worst Story Told Of My Life

The worst story told of my life was not the meeting of you with me!!

But the worst is you forgot,
but am unable to forget...
mine that time —
and that phase of mine.
Girl!!
I thought that —
time has the "token" to forget you,
and too... has a destination of happiness for me.

But everything went wrong!!
and now in my empty hands...
I have a memory of you —
and has a tear of me.

Every Sunset Has A Modest Feel For The Night

Every sunset has a modest feel for the night...

I too have the same...
no matter that you tried your best,
to stab me,
even with a blunt knife!!

I won't... and, I don't have any issues, Girl!!
that there were no notifications... that I am being hated by you!!
and you began to hate me,
just as a wine hates the consciousness of mind!!

But I promise!!
that one day... you loved me or not –
it won't matter to me!!
But –
there will always be...
an audition of talent in me,
of,
how much I loved you!!
and even till now...
how much you are being loved,
as heartily in me, as you will always be mine.

Just as an optimist has wide-open eyes,
without closing...
so, the inclination of the pupil by default catches, more light,
and thus, the light of life...
same thing, the hope of you is so divine.

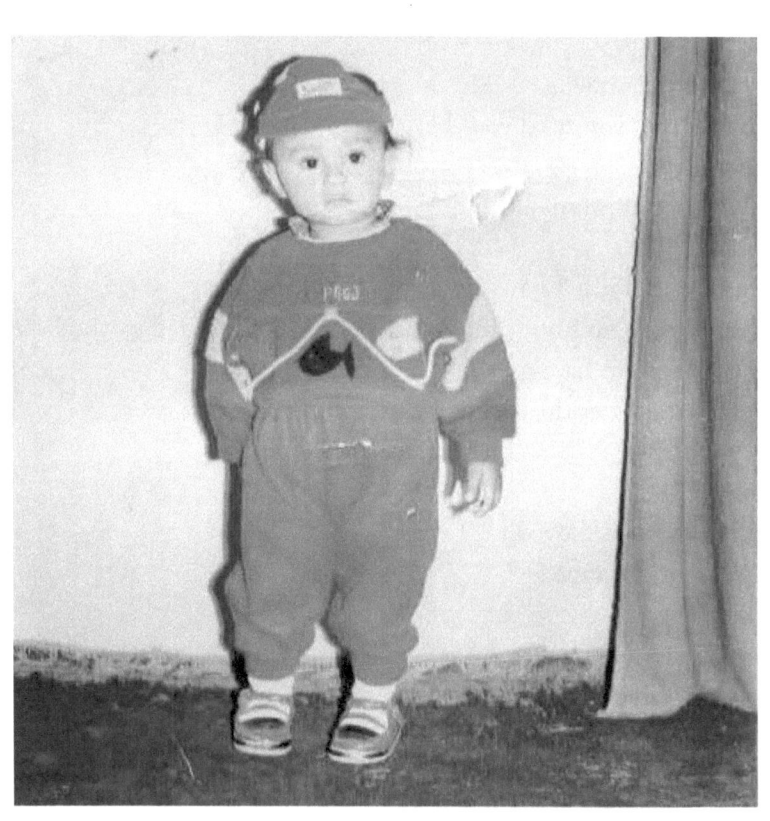

My childhood pic

The In-Love Cuteness Of A Child

A good person is who???

Who puts even his garbage separately,
on a cleaner surface, with an intention...
so that a starving dog or a cow,
can feed on it!!
without soil, gravel or concrete.

If he has an abundance of cockroaches in his house,
then in the feeling to get rid of...
and also, with the feeling of pity!!
he urgently brings "BAYGON" with his own pocket money...
and spreads that on every cockroach!!
so that, by the next day...
they cannot give birth to the "new ones,"
and those newborn infants!!
at least may not feel the certain dilemma of death and pain... as their parents did!!

A butterfly, when seemed with broken wings and crawling like a miniature reptile!!
rather than to just pass by,
crushes him totally like making it a powder,
to curtail the excruciating death time.
So that small ants... in N numbers, may not nibble on hers every possible part,
and she should not bear that unbearable pain...
when she is certain to die.

In his mind with sadness, committing a sin, but...
in the first thought, the butterfly was euthanized.

And Baby!!
at least that person, who even in a huge rush for his urinal!!
opens the door quickly,
but by seeing the —
"Innocent commode-settled ants,"
feeding on sugary residue...
gives a warning of two-three drops,
so that —
before the tsunami of his own, burst banks!!
would cause severe damage or death,
to them and their relatives,
they can escape from there,
in the meantime.

And hey, Girl!!
believe me, I was one of that kind :(.
Then say...
why you left me???
when even mom says...
"Good things happen, to good people, who are good and kind."

Then say...
why did you leave me???
when I was so innocent, sincere, and naive humankind.

Revision Itself Is A New Course Of Persistence

Because,
the end of fumble is too crucial of an elegance.

Sometimes rather than a new study or a new course,
sometimes revision is the best upgrade that you can have.

Every information is to be pulled from recycle bin to the main brain,
so, that you can blurt,
latent informative information...
with much more confidence.

We Don't Have To Narrate First, We Just Have To Make Our Stories

Emotions have great possibilities,
extremely, they can sink...
and extremely, they can culminate the bearer,
to the great accessibilities.

Mediocrity is when...
we got or behaved with emotions ordinarily.
So, live with and accelerate in it wisely.

Because...
something is in effect,
something is in defect,
in sync with life's glee and melancholy.

We don't have to narrate,
first, we just have to make our stories.

Thus,
being emotional one should become more of...
one's own gravity.
It's ok if you have high estrogen or testosterone levels,
for better and best reasons,
perhaps not only for sex or adultery,
but for many other good and efficient...
regarding the aspect of productivity.

So and so is crucial to remember...
fascinating things happen to them,
who have fascinations with their so-called dreams,
and thus,
"Law of attraction" directs them,
according to their believed audacity.

Better Are The Times I Show Not Even My Fangs And The Foe Persuades

Incompetency has been sculpted and eliminated from me, that's why better I'm seemingly to myself...
forget about the world, they are perceiving the same.

Nonetheless with the instances of the past... with my brain, I want to walk alone,
better are the times, I show not even my fangs and the foe persuades...
I am something with the judgment of myself,
the stillness and turmoil are better managed.
The daydreaming in myself is something, that enthrals me much more than a sci-fi movie,
before achieving that or not... before that too I enjoy the insanity,
which even before the commencement, to myself, I claimed.

Sorry, your brain doesn't support... that chip given to or gifted or specially honed...
for me, that's mundane.

Endeavours of mine are not one,
endeavours of mine are much more as I am sane,
I am a writer and a lifter...
distractions worked on me; now it's time to gain,
cumulatively from the same, moreover, much more...
me belonging or being something soon is as suitable as,
ashes are never broken, they are burnt,
the truth for something never changes.

Mysteriously, the things seem captivating,
that's why unique things are claimed...
my life is not and will not be a fiasco,
two-three likes would not ever define me,
introvert I am, but bestselling would be my life's fame.
Never a seeker of attention because it hinders my most precious and loved seclusion,
but,
omnipresent will be my name...
it is to happen; I cannot be tamed.

So, Have Experience Of Humans, Yes Read Them

Everything is an experience:
fierce, middle, meagre, or negligent,
so,
somehow, anyhow, be an observer.

Sometimes time management is extremely intense,
so, have experience of humans,
yes, read them...
they are the ones who wrote the books,
and say, just like only paperback readings are helpful for mental acuity and all,
I would say that's good, but...
it's more efficient without getting complications,
than to have the past scribbled things,
do the live things...
because in that, no time management or aura of library is needed to sit and swot,
freely you can have hyperplasia of brain cells :),
even in whatever restricted ages :).
Come on!!
when you have the Creator himself around you,
revolving and evolving around you...
in each and every nuance of life making up stories,
optionally and exactly so, many times...
there is nothing being to be much enthralling,
in the same human's creativity,
and his contorted or perverted made-up stories.
It's too entertaining,

rather than nothing, come on, accept it!!
humans are concealed containing gist,
alike books... immortal books,
texture and each and every layer of these fellow mortals containing them are too enticing.

The Eureka Moment

The Eureka moment, or a bit of enlightenment is...
when you will be in your zone,
time would be yours to elapse...
acting to impress others would be less.
You will feel more comfortable in a new concentration,
and rather than the whole, a concise thing would be more impressive
in public and solicitation.

All good...
but it's a different designation.

When Meaningless Are The Altercations

When meaningless are the altercations,
in reference to relevant,
then obscure should be the things.

Better, let's give room for the confusion.

Everything is Copied

Everything is copied in this world...
until and unless it hasn't the "copyright."

Just as the word called "life,"
which I am too living since my birth,
and as someone... has lived it already!!

So yup :),
I am a copy-cat.

My biggest supporter Maa...

Happy Mother's Day

I never had told her or dictated her to behave decently,
nevertheless, she always did... and still does,
and when she doesn't... it's understood :).

She is humane and is filled with affection,
but her silence sometimes says and instils fear in me that,
she doesn't want,
but nevertheless imminently...
she will ruin my mind,
as when I had broken a flower vase,
while trying a sport.
When she shouted not to cross the threshold...
due to some unknown reasons...
even that was the routine of weekend or Sunday jubilation,
no doubt I was conscious enough, but don't know how that ball jumped!
advertently, much more unexpected,
even being non-living too... in the game,
in return incurred extra sentences.

In my exams,
she murmurs blessings...
in a way that a God from Earth is applying an application to consider
and further,
to the God in the sky.
I never topped... but every time got marks beyond my expectations —
extra or grace marks because of someone's grace.

She owns tears because of me,
and smiles often because of me...

she is the only sacred relation,
which I will not find anywhere else,
that gave birth to me.
My heart hides my sorrows...
but if she even gets a bit of a clue,
that I am in a bit of it,
then until she knows the whole...
she is irritated by reiterating,
and unless she knows,
she behaves restless and she even sleeps restlessly,
with much more apprehensions and anguish.

Her scolds are meaningful,
and her praises are priceless...
she may nitpick, aptly like others,
but every time deliberately... she neglects.

Many times, I have opened my eyes...
as usual,
and found my mother even in her sleeping state,
was giving light strokes with her fingers, on my head...
I said irritated, "You sleep *naa*...,"
but internally thanked her fondness.

She always says I am a gem...
a precious gem for her,
I smiled and never bothered,
by giving an example too...
that "what is she for me?"
because somewhere she is beyond the examples or metaphors to be used,
for what I may explain... for the explanations which can brief or elaborate.

She smiles still after three decades,
and until she will...
she beseeches me still... to listen,
those interesting tales, (according to her),
that how my childhood was.

Well, some of my bit favourites!!
my gestures when I got irritated,
or pout due to some whims or craves,
about that disloyal bird in whose injury,
and unfortunate time I fed,
which flew... when she felt perked,
without thanking me.

And then too, after this deception too...
how me and my friends...
had made a cemented small room,
and then too after this deception too...
fed that loyal dog... named "Kaalu,"
who strayed and left his father-mother...
because of the complaint never told,
but understood –
(as somewhere it was written on his face),
that they were affectionless.

We even gave him Cadbury Eclairs toffees...
without knowing then that they don't have much enzymes, to digest
those kinds...
and began to lose his hairs,
because of us, day and night!!
even in the caprice (he too has the right to taste well),
how I bought Pedigree from my pocket money...
and sometimes because of him when I involved myself in nefarious
activities, and surreptitiously even picked up coins from shelves,

and much more...
ufff... I am bored of them,
I never did even for myself — to steal even for the cakes, which I loved heartedly for myself,
but don't know how the dog "Kallu" found,
every time in those same things... a new taste, and as I was not earning, it became a chain!!
May be his tongue was new,
only a few months back that grew,
that's why even a paper might be to his palatable not so much of a bad taste,
but don't know how does she finds, in those anecdotes,
every time it has a new taste...
well, these are only some anecdotes which are my favourite...
she has infinitely many more to envisage.

She had a stash of cookies and namkeens...
which she bought,
not many times but... each and every time,
that bought saliva even after my full night meals,
but she never gave me meaninglessly,
until that was a marked time.
I thought at that point of childhood...
and when I was a toddler,
that she was rude...
but today I can understand that I was senseless,
and she was aware of my appetite...
and had conscience,
that, what should I eat and at what time.
Now,
I am bigger than her... and now today,
I am taller than her size,
but she still suggests what should I wear,
and declares as if a diktat that,

it would be fine.
I respect her from the bottom of my heart...
and sometimes she becomes unruly,
(too is a point).
Nevertheless —
I am adherent to those adamant statements...
as much as possible,
like a senseful but in front of her,
idiot, foolish in almost not every case, but summarized.

Now there are "Kinder Joy",
and much more kinds of different joys for children,
but I enjoyed other means of joy...
which were relevant at that point of time,
and she still through those makes me nostalgic,
I can enjoy my memories...
and my mom's repeated delight.
Like an unsolved puzzle, but even when I was unable to walk or tell anything,
how she solved my untold beautiful maze...
what I wanted or on what I got irritated,
to find out everything about me,
was her most dedicated game.
She is special beyond my lifetime too because...
no one has ever the best recording with my wholesome to toddler to even day one,
or of whatever phase...
no one is that much interested,
and I know no one would be...
the capacity of her is gospel truth and undenied.

You Are A Girl, Be In A Safe Zone, Safe Side

Times and moments which I had with you were umpteen,
that's why,
in my each and every hour (reluctantly even), there is a share of thoughts still related to you.

Girl, I even vowed... many a time,
and I was supposed to do something else, like omitting you...
and I am doing something else again, like remembering you.

Because till today, months have turned up into years...
I'm not capable of ousting you,
from that position,
to being in leisure and solace... I should oust you.

Despondency of life is due to you... (it's true),
but what I lost... till today,
and till today... what I am losing,
you should know...
that is nothing in front of what I got from you.

Tears trickle down on your every single memory,
disclosing those known feelings that, once upon a time I had a special person like you...
that's enough reason I think why I owe you too,
because somewhere it's the fact that,
I experienced the magic of true and first love only with the involvement (and due to you).

And if...
in the vagaries of life today,
you are giving me only pain (which pains a lot),
(When compared to your decent memories,
decent face, and decent manners of you).

Nevertheless, for this meagre and mere reason only,
rather I will pay the cost of still loving you,
but I'm not going to exile or erase you.
My broken heart is like May-June's torrid Thar desert... (devoid of life).
Near and dear ones say,
"Nothing is left there, move on..."
because there is not even a bit of a worthy lively drop,
then too... neglecting the certain environs of Oasis outside...
it's my internal desire,
that is for the craving of life... I have to live,
because there is still hope amidst,
that one day you would know that,
in me, how much you were revered...
and still how much you are being loved.

Because what to do!!
life is destined to dream and my desire as was always and still is, to be with you.
(Whether it's a mirage... and the whole story from your side is nothing).
Nevertheless, as a corpse... I have to show you.

Two things may or might happen after such a long duration...
and according to these aspects of you.

(Firstly), whether my heart, rambling with me,
falls in love with every girl who seems like you.

(Secondly), I am still obsessed with the thoughts of you...
and my lips smile still in the memories of you.

Remember first one is not true; second one is true.
I am not bored with the same depict and same descriptions of that
person's face, gestures, innate modesty, behaviours, instincts, etc.,
that had enthralled me,
from her first glance and her first view.

Whom I loved truly from the bottom of my heart,
even if I haven't confronted her for years,
and there is nothing new.

But at last, my beloved...!!
at the endless wait...
if the conclusion God would give to my story, or to me would be the
mirage case,
and if till date you had or have concocted,
that you haven't or hadn't felt a jot of something for me,
and that there was nothing between us more than some exchanges of
gaze...
(because everything is unknown to the world that what was our
internal heartily case).

Then again what to do?
(it affects me) but what to do?

You are a girl... be in a safe zone, safe side,
if now I am a nerd and if it embarrasses you,
then too... I will not ever condemn you.

Because then too I would love to love you,
as a person you were...

rather who, on your own volition, is masquerading as you,
and again... I know then too I have my treasure in me with me...
because again :),
I am not bored with the same depict and same descriptions of that
person's face, gestures, innate modesty, behaviours, instincts, etc., etc.,
that had enthralled me,
from her first glance and her first view.

Whom I loved truly from the bottom of my heart...
whether I haven't confronted her for years,
and there is nothing new.
As I aforesaid... (which you can review).

But please... tell or please say, from whatever source you want,
at least as a friend, that...
when in every drizzling weather of emotions...
my life and I will continue to feel emotions related to you,
and at the same time vice versa...
the mourns of not being with you,
then how would I generalize internally with...
the moist droplets on my eyelashes each such that —
my tears are emotionally related to you still,
but I'm not involved in remembering you,
and Girl, I have no veneration still related...
or being directly neglected,
the recurring feelings of that person...
who still at present, has its importance more than me in me,
and in bed without suffering from insomnia...
I slept a wholesome cozy sleep,
without wasting a second on you.

At least a person who knows me more than me or like me was you...
and I think somewhere that is still you,

and you know that —
I could or would never want to pester you,
whether today, that is emotionally,
but I am not asking for myself...
it's for that person in me who is so innocuous, poor, and naive...
that even I am feeling pity for him,
regarding his case.

And my tears are oozing out for the reason,
that, why I have had such a veneration for you...
that why you changed so bizarrely,
and my feelings remained so immutable for you,
say Girl, say from whatever source you want to.

When you were destined to give him pain,
then why did you become so pretty...
that you are so inevitable still as a recurring thought,
that in the worst conditions too,
he is unable to retort to you...
or to feelings related to you that get lost...!!
I don't need you... I don't even want you...!!

I am in tears...
say Girl, say from whatever source you want to.

It's his problem...
but please as a friend solve it up to that extent...
up to which it is needed to.

Say Girl, say from whatever source you want to,
say Girl, say from whatever source you want to.

It's my problem...

but please as a friend solve it up to that extent...
up to which it is needed to.

Say Girl, say from whatever source you want to,
say Girl, say from whatever source you want to.

I Never Gloated You, Below Your Neckline

Not only tears were,
or are the most precious thing,
which I had lost in the memories of you,
from when you had denied.
Every desire of mine too... for life plummeted,
like a star plummets, from the sky,
after completing his life.

And I was so in trance, so much in pain,
that I forgot to wish from that star...
according to Katrina Kaif of "Ajab Prem ki Ghazab Kahani,"
in the relation of desires of mine,
maybe then too, I cared about a question,
that by doing that you will be mine!!
but if you didn't want it, then?
because I was not of your kind,
so, for your happiness... I didn't,
and instead of that —
like other broken heart guys in my town,
whom I had seen...
I opted for —
A Bacardi bottle,
so, that the severe pain given by you,
may quench under the inebriation of that wine.

But see!!
that time whizzed past,
like a steady stroll of someone converts meters into miles...

nevertheless, pain is still that much —
like (train) PRAYAG RAJ since years or decades, I think,
is commuting and as well as completing,
his mundane job —
from Allahabad to this city of mine.

And my situation is still alike!!
like a stinted piece of cloth or a tatter on a twig,
fluttering in the presence of whizz-passing winds,
and then too can't cross...
even an inch of its ambits.

By the way by seeing or observing internally,
meanwhile —
a cyclone of thoughts hits my human mind...
and then a panorama of your memory with me,
begins to rewind.

That —
how your two smug eyes rested,
beneath those two beautiful eyebrows of yours,
when your attention was weak —
as you were concentrated on a topic of creed...
I simply and sincerely stared at you,
and never disclosed what I had,
observed of you.
The strands of your hair which came on your left cheek,
between this observation of mine...
how they told me about the contrast of your skin,
that interruption was too soothing of an experience,
which I never wanted to kill.

Your innocent gestures between the truce with you and someone's,

before that, whatever was the strife,
told me about your humane approach...
even for those —
who doesn't have the guts to confront you,
or struggle to thrive.

The light rings which you occasionally had on your nose,
sorry, I don't know what may I say those in English,
but I heard somewhere,
that, that is called "Nathni" in Hindi.
By the way...!!
Yes... that when combined —
with mild smiles or occasionally with me,
a candid hilarious wide smile,
in confabs of you and mine...
was like a certain auspicious sign for me,
like somewhere a seer has prognosticated directly,
that my whole day will be full of mundane jubilation,
as you were my sunshine.
 I experienced that tickle,
even when your face buzzed...
whether sometimes that was my siesta,
or whenever that was a nocturnal sleep of mine.
By the way —
I don't have much ink and pages will be less to describe,
well, this one is too...
the largest poem which I'm writing in my life,
but in my observations do you know???
I never gloated you, below your neckline,
because I was in true love from one side!!

But today a mischievous guy...
posted mischievously on my Facebook timeline,

that you are going to marry, someone soon,
which I aptly hid on time.
Why is not a question... but the trouble is!!
someone great said that —
"When you revere something, with a true heart,
then the whole universe conspires,"
then why is God not on my side???
why you are opting for that opulent guy!
neglecting my lifestyle...
 you will smile with him!
only because I'm not settled, that's why???

It's only a subtle or meagre truth,
that in my life I saw a person like you,
but it's more spectacular and prominent truth,
that in my life whom I met,
I loved her weirdly...
whether that was you.
I will prove it to you...
whether you had somehow, somewhere,
deliberately neglected me.

But what will you think of me after even decades...
whether that will be relevant or irrelevant,
unless neglected —
it will always matter to me.
Bruises given by you are special,
and will always be —
like you were special,
whether you gave them deliberately or inadvertently.

Every sweet confab of us... in which,
there is a delicacy of your thoughts and voice,

will not become a rustle...
it will remain as it was... or as it is today.
A lonely place for me will be my lonely mind,
(without you),
which is and will be an impossible thing.

As experiences of mine are not limited about you...
every subtle detail of you...
the description which depicts,
while undergoing through... that what were you,
will not ever become...
a silhouette for me.

Nothing ever will be new,
but I will think like — quake came with an intensity of 7.9,
and by chance, we were in a ramshackle building,
which became a multitude of only red rubbles...
within a tick of time,
but as the disaster management chapter had told us,
and as you were prudent...
we were under a firm furniture reclined.

Everything was heavenly before my death,
until God came garbed in Army dress,
with stars on his epaulettes,
and with a lady doctor with a handbag of {+} sign.

To whom I disclosed,
that extremely auspicious or fortunate thing,
happened how atrociously and unfortunately,
on brink of my death and on verge of my life,
while I was staring at a subtle wound on your shin,
and then in your eyes.

And Girl!!
thus, many artificial anecdotes would be made, inspired by real ones, and...
I will continue it, till my entire life.

I Don't Write Generally
"Main Aksar Likhta Nahi"
In The Whole Lot, You Know A Jot Of Only This.

Girl, you don't know anything,
as such... you just seem that...
likely everything is seen,
and everything is in front of you,
but you know a jot, not a lot...
I have written many books,
you just know a book titled,
say — "Main Aksar Likhta Nahi."
Nothing else like content or few!!

That's like the same,
like you know, "I am just inclined to you."
(This book has),
"Main Aksar Likhta Nahi,"
of which you know the title only,
that Vishal Sarkar has written a book!!
but —
it has 168 names of poems and phrases on the list... not known anything about to you,
then, 168 poems and phrases have actually with each title on each one of the list,
confabulating and disclosing 168 types of emotions and a variety of nuances and touching,
which you didn't read,
and so subtle and diverse that each one opens up a different best in each reputation of reading.

So Girl, just knowing...
"*Main Aksar Likhta Nahi,*"
"I don't write generally,"
as a title.

I have written...
1)- *Main Aksar Likhta Nahi,*
2)- *Isliye Hi Shayad,*
3)- *Khair Fir Bhi,*
4)- *Kuch Fitoor Bus,* etc.,
and in English,
5)- Tunes of Time... Incessant You.
👇 👇 👇 👇
Say these five —
and in these five, you know just the title of the first written...
not even a quarter of the page.
My emotions are the same in front of you,
but actually, and factually...
my emotions for you are like...
168 pages each × 5 = 840 pages.

Now see 1 quarter of not even a page versus 840 pages.
So, let's take... 1 whole page, divided by 840×100 = 0.119047619%,
not even one single percent is known by you!!

How minuscule like you are in minutes versus an aeon to you,
like you know versus you don't know to you,
in how someone at an instinct is bound to feel about you...
latent, hidden, profoundly compressed, and not opening up to you.
That's the depth of the ocean and in my concerns,
in which I love you.

A Note From The Author

If not that much impressive then,
it's their lower IQ,
that they can't or don't understand the level,
the benchmark of the upper... lustre and radiance.

It's their insensitive, emotionless, degraded sense of conscience, and inclination,
that they can't go to the aisle,
where for the best experience,
I guided them to have a pristine to modern residence.

Sorry, no audacity but...
otherwise, for the rest, accolades...
and praises, I praise and thank you 💝.
Which states that whatever the font size,
but inch by inch...
with full conscious attention to imbibe,
my words, sentences and gist are impeccable.
Whatever I wanted to emote on the brochure or chart as deliverables :),
no hype,
moreover... they got the physical touch like in the mind utmost,
as the view,
as the conclusion is considerate, natural, not artificially synthesized.

www.ingramcontent.com/pod-product-compliance
Lightning Source LLC
LaVergne TN
LVHW091624070526
838199LV00044B/918